WALKING THROUGH THE FLAMES

The First Step into Hell

Carol Tuttle

Library of Congress Control Number:		2007903681
ISBN:	Hardcover	978-1-4257-6439-5
	Softcover	978-1-4257-6425-8

This book was printed in the United States of America.

To order additional copies of this book, contact:
Xlibris Corporation
1-888-795-4274
www.Xlibris.com
Orders@Xlibris.com
40297

WALKING THROUGH THE FLAMES

CONTENTS

INTRODUCTION

As you pick up this book and thumb through it, you may be thinking, "Oh heck, another autobiography by another nobody." True, it's my life and my various experiences, yet it is in many ways everybody's life; perhaps not in total, yet here and there you may find yourself. It is the story of child abuse, spousal abuse, and the abuse of children who are products of that union.

To me the words put down on these pages are very important, as I am the one who bears the physical and emotional scars, which are finally in the deep process of healing. It's really everybody's story in one way or another, how I was able to overcome the dark side. Some never recover; I believe I am and have. In one way or another and throughout its length this story was written to convey the message that we all suffer to one degree or another, yet we can overcome and survive, making us stronger, better people.

It is the story of an unyielding faith in a Power beyond that of this earth, a faith to which I was born and which was developed and encouraged, mostly by my immigrant Italian grandparents, a faith which has seen me through the most critical times.

My path led me to a broad path of deep Catholicism via the meeting of people like Jose Silva and his transcendental expansion. He, among so many beautiful others, had given me insight into myself and a different perspective of the facets of my life in general. I am convinced that all is never lost. There will always be a tomorrow.

There is an expression of the existence of God, yet in a "New Age" way of seeing Him. Being eclectic, I've found it comfortable to be able to grow into and toward the future and yet continue holding onto the old ways, creating for me a balance in my faith. I have often fallen off my path and true calling, but by an act of grace, have always been brought back.

God has never deserted me—or you. You may not have faith in Him, yet He has always been with us all, waiting patiently for us to turn to Him for acknowledgment and acceptance.

It is my belief that each of us has lived other lifetimes—a multiplicity—and on that theme further writings will be forthcoming. Our consciousness carries with it, upon birth, the knowledge of those other lives (ever hear of "deja vu"?) and therefore, calling it Karma (the way our past lives follow us) or Dharma (the work on the paths in this lifetime), our paths, our lifetimes are predestined. We have lessons to learn so we will not have to repeat them. We then expand our souls, our spirits to and for better things to come.

I have encountered, along my path, the beautiful peace-loving Dali Lama, the Maharashi, and many others. One incident found me at a moonlit circle in a forest accompanied by eleven other women and a warlock. I have tasted the cup of the negativity of life including the Clare Prophet cult, etc.—all cults. Not my way. I have become a master teacher of Usui Reiki, thereby empowering and giving me more of the taste of honey, although I am the first to admit I have no power, only the openness and willingness to allow myself to become an instrument, to be used whenever and wherever I am and have been needed, always looking for the soul, not seeing race, creed, or color.

I have searched my whole life for the comforting hand of another human—never there! Yet I persist. Perhaps one day! God is the one Being who has remained faithful to me, as I have been to Him. He is the only one who has ever been there for me when I would reach out for help. I have always had His guidance to pick me up whenever I have fallen and to set me back on the path whenever I have strayed.

Life has not been easy, but I guess I didn't ask for an easy life before I was born. I do not sit in judgment on those who seem "to have it all," for who knows what is lacking in their lives? I certainly have lacked for very little in the way of experiences in my life.

I have loved and felt rejection. I have experienced molestation and depredation. I have also known kindness. I have experienced out-and-out brutality. Yet I have known love. It has all been worth the price I have had to pay. I have learned to paint a smile on my face—close the door behind me and face the world—never letting anyone know the physical or emotional pain inside myself.

I have learned to forgive without forgetting; I have felt forgiveness being returned by way of love. Perhaps not the love I have been searching for, but there has been love returned.

This book is a message for all who wish to be survivors. We can all transcend our difficulties. May this book become a little guide for you. I state this in all humbleness and humility.

May God be with us all and
"Thank you for this moment."

With the writing of this book, and the telling the world of my history, I shall be attempting to bring to an end the pathos of an entire lifetime. May this become the catharsis for which I've been searching. Until I had gotten deeply into this book, and with the trust guidance of my mentor, I had no idea how inhibited I had become. This, too, is changing. My entire world is doing a complete turnaround. As has been said, "When one door closes, another quickly opens."

My mentor, and my beloved friend, opened the door for me and with strength of compassion saw me through and walked me through the painful paces, making me not only face, but accept things that I thought had been long hidden and locked away from even myself. He helped me open old wounds and release the years of festering within so I can now heal. I don't mind the scars left behind for they are proof of what made me the person I am today. This is only a new beginning, and with many thanks, I say, "God bless you too," as He has blessed me in leading me to and opening door to freedom."

Carol

CHAPTER I

From End to Beginning

No one will ever convince me there is no God, and that He doesn't keep our Guardian Angels watching over us.

> "... *He will protect us like a bird spreading its wings over its young. He has put his Angels in charge of us. They will watch over us wherever we go, They will catch us with their hands . . .*"
> Psalm #91: "The Everyday Bible"

We stood up, as though on command, in unison, not saying a word, just the three of us. Suddenly we stood and took a couple of steps away from our seats, and stopped just as suddenly, looking at the coffin. There were very few flowers and even fewer people present. Who the hell was in the coffin? My mother.

She lived in a bubble called Mildred, for herself and by herself, and now that bubble had been placed into an oak box with brass fittings, ready to be buried six feet underground. Through the last five or six years of her life she had eventually become trapped in her own mind with her own demons. She had become more vicious toward my father and often did not even recognize him. Yet when I arrived daily after work to prepare their meals, pick up their laundry and straighten out the house, she always knew who I was and what I was doing. Strange, how she never seemed to forget who I was. She would eat and then go into the bathroom and vomit it back. My sister and I believed she had become anorexic. She was always afraid of putting on weight, and to the very end she was convinced she had the greatest body and legs a woman could want. Mother believed there was a woman who lived upstairs with three children, and often, over coffee, she would suddenly jump up, grab a dish towel from the counter and scrub an imaginary spot on the kitchen floor. I'd ask, "Mother, what are you doing?" as one would speak softly to a child. Her answer was always, "Can't you see what that kid did, pissing on the floor?" I'd quietly say, "It's all right, Mother, it's clean now." Her answer was always the same: "Oh, all right," and she'd set the towel back on the counter and come back and sit down, losing herself again in another part of her mind. Meanwhile, Dad and I would continue on with our conversation. There were those few, brief occasions when she'd get a faraway look on her face, almost peaceful, and Dad and I would stop talking, just watching her. Wherever her mind had taken her, we didn't want to interrupt. But she usually came back with a vengeance, as if distraught over the loss of those wondrous thoughts. There were other times she'd either reach out to punch Dad or give him a powerful kick in the shins. I'd calmly place my hand on her arm and tell her, "Mother, it's all right, it's Dad." Often she came back with the nasty voice, "Can't you see what he's doing with that woman?" "It's all right, Mother, she's gone now. She won't come back." It was heartbreaking to watch Mother drowning mentally as well as physically.

After checking her medication to be certain she'd taken her daily supply, it was time for me to leave, and I always gave her a hug and a kiss on the cheek and tell her, "I love you, Mother. Have a peaceful night and please get some sleep so Dad can rest." She'd never answer or return my kiss and hug. As old as I'd become, I still wanted that hug, that show of affection.

Tonight at Mother's wake, all I could see of that cadaverous body was her large, sharply pointed nose, protruding above the coffin. I must be in the wrong room. That ugly creature can't be my mother, who so often reminded me of how beautiful she was, that same person I never wanted any part of me to be like. She never could do her own hair; we had to do it. She never took care of her nails, which is probably why I let mine grow so long (and always have, since I was a high school freshman) and take good care of them. She never knew fashion; we had to dress her. She never wore a bra; we wouldn't be caught dead without one. So who was this body who was so emaciated, to the point of being shaped like an ironing board? She was never without a drink in her hand, God forbid, through the years we were growing up; we don't imbibe. She never wanted to become pregnant and have brats hanging off of her and, consequently, she never allowed any of us to sit in her lap, never gave us a hug; we love our children, and the times when we were with child were truly the happiest days of our lives. She never kept a clean house; we are meticulous. She never knew how to cook; we are skilled cooks. And she always nagged. Poor Dad. We are not nags. She didn't like or trust many people; we have many friends and love many people. And she never was hygienically clean; we are all meticulous and scrupulously clean. She always coveted anything anyone had, including her daughters, anything they thought were their treasures; it mattered not how trivial. And last, but certainly not least, she lived 88 years without ever having learned how to give or receive love.

I don't think she believed in God; she simply lived in her own world, for herself only and for what she could acquire. It would never have occurred to my mother to make a pot of stew to take to a sick neighbor. Thank you, God, for raising us above all that she was, by teaching us that you exist.

I looked around me. Yes, there was my husband, my children, my father, and to my right, my always beautiful, well-coifed, red-headed oldest sister, Edda. Then to my left, my beautiful, ethereal, not-quite-of-this-world sister Nancy, whose glorious mane of honey-colored hair tonight looked dead, like the bristles of a broom. Her features were still ethereal, but I thought she looked as bad as the thing in the coffin. And suddenly I realized she had worn red, scarlet red, lip-liner, penciled in where her eyebrows were supposed to be. It was only the fifth or sixth time I had seen her since she had gone west in the early 1950s. The once flawless, porcelain-like skin was weathered and worn; the beautiful dancing brown eyes glazed over, as though her mind and thoughts were not quite with us. It was a surrealistic sight; it was all wrong, and I thought, it must be my medication.

It had been only 48 hours since my angioplasty and my stent had been put in. What I was seeing and feeling that night at Mother's wake was not real. There was not a tear or a sob from any one of the three of us. We simply stood there, like wooden statues, unwilling to witness this scene or give in to it or to pray her a goodbye as was our custom.

After what seemed an eternity, we stepped back and seated ourselves again. I have no way of knowing what ran through my sisters' minds. I thought, "thank God it's almost over." And my thoughts once again turned to my sister Nancy, on my right. It was June, 1998. It was quite warm and I don't even recall what my sisters or I were wearing. I only felt relief that this part of my ordeal was about over. There was only tomorrow's funeral to face. I do recall it was extremely hot and uncomfortable. There was no eulogy spoken at Mother's or Dad's funerals. I do feel guilty over that. To me it is not trivial—more of a travesty. Both had private funerals—family only.

My memory went back to 1956 again. Nancy and her husband Bob, who had been in the Air Force based in occupied Japan, had returned from the west coast with a little baby boy. Nancy had gotten a secretarial job on Travis Air Force Base and had remained behind when Bob was shipped overseas. The story they had agreed on was that a girl Nancy worked with had had this child but couldn't keep him; therefore, Nancy and Bob had agreed to adopt him and bring him back to Connecticut with them. Ironically, my fear was that upon their return, Nancy, whom I had always loved dearly and looked up to, would reject me, as I was a now-unwed mother. My son was five months old, her baby was three months old.

One afternoon, soon after they arrived in Connecticut, Nancy visited me at our mother's house, where I still lived, and after we chatted about the nothings of life our babies awoke. Time to change and feed them. My baby's crib was in the dining room of the house; I was then sleeping on the sofa in the living room, only a few feet away from him. I would not sleep upstairs and leave him downstairs away from me; there was no heat upstairs, and it was too cold for a little baby. Nancy and I smiled, and as we laid our babies on their receiving blankets on the dining room table to change them, I quite naturally asked her, "Was it a difficult birth for you?" She quietly said, "No. It was easy." Without another word we picked up one another's babies and hugged them to our breasts, as though sharing one another's sadness and love. Then, holding the babies, we hugged each other. The only important thing at that moment was that we still loved one another, no questions needed to be asked, or answered.

With squirming, crying, hungry babies in our arms, reluctantly we broke away from the comfort we were giving one another, and I'm certain my face carried as much concern and worry as did hers—not so much for our babies, but for our tomorrows, so many yesterdays, yet so many tomorrows ahead to face. We wiped our tears with the backs of our hands, smiled knowingly at each other, and proceeded through the archway of the dining room into the living room, to feed our sons.

For me, Nancy will always look as she did at that moment, holding her son, feeding him, bearing her ethereal yet perfectly porcelain beautiful face with love. God had truly blessed her with an angelic face of perfection, viewed from any angle. That was my Nancy at that moment. Tonight was not the Nancy of my memory. Tonight she was a stranger.

That afternoon, she quietly said to me, "Carrie, I have a favor to ask of you. There is a gentleman named Bill who is my baby's father, and who followed Bob and me across the country, he's staying in a local hotel. Will you go to him and let him know the baby and I will go back to the West Coast with him?" I looked at her, and said, "Nancy, you can't do that. Bob is willing to accept and raise this baby as his own. He has a good job, he can give you all of the comforts and all of the peace you want in life." She said, "But I don't love Bob. I love Bill." I said, "Why don't you love Bob?" And she replied, "Because he doesn't hurt me." I didn't understand at that moment what she meant. It was many years before I had read and studied enough psychology to understand that my beautiful sister Nancy did not know how to make love, give love, without being hurt—physically injured—in the process. And I felt her problems were my own at that precise moment.

How much I have always loved my sisters, especially this one, with whom now I shared so much growing up, the one over whom I had felt the greatest loss when she had been moved to a foster home away from me. Watching her, my mind went back to that horrendous nightmare, which seemed a lifetime ago. She was 15 and I was 11. Edda had already been moved to a foster home, and that night, when Nancy had been out babysitting, I had awakened to Mother's shouts of "Beat it out of her, Nick! Make her tell us where she's been and what she's been doing!" I ran downstairs to see my dad punch Nancy, as Mother seemed eager and excited, screaming, "Who've you been with? What have you been doing?" inciting my father to hit Nancy again and again, which he did until his last punch threw her from the kitchen through the doorway up against the dining room wall under the window across the house. It was 2:00 a.m. I don't recall Nancy ever attempting to even utter any kind of explanation or plea. There wasn't time; it all happened so fast. Dad, in his youth, had been a Golden Gloves boxer, and this beating occurred long before the law had been passed that a boxer's hands were lethal weapons. My beautiful little Nancy, lying in a little heap of swelling, with blood running over her face, as I ran crying to her, hearing my dad say, "Jesus Christ, Mildred—I think I've killed her!" Crying, I called her name. "Nancy! Nancy!" And she weakly opened her eyes, ever so slightly, and said in a whisper, through swollen, bloody lips, "Carrie, save yourself." Then her head slumped at an odd angle, as my mother grabbed me by the upper arm and threw me through that archway, up against that same sofa upon which I now sat feeding my baby, hollering at me to get away from my sister. Dad drove to pick up my mother's mother, my beloved Grams, and they took Nancy to the hospital. I didn't see her again until she was ready to get married, after high school. So here we were, same place, different time, sharing even more pain. Was it ever to end? Perhaps in my case, it will finally end one day soon.

It did not end the day after Mother's wake when she was buried. The emotional wounds never really healed, but I believe, with God's help, they will now. At least they will scar over and the past will be over and done with.

Seated on the sofa that day in 1956, I glanced around me. Dad's boxing gloves, which always hung in the corner between the dining room and the living room, were missing, and I looked toward my right, the north wall, where Mother had hung a small plaque when we were very young, bearing a poem that began, "Father is the Captain of our family ship." They were missing. The refrigerator and the sewing machine were still in the same place—Nancy lay between them that night—and I wondered, what else is missing? Then I knew: the days when I should have been allowed to be a little girl. My childhood. Our childhood. Mother had taken those away from us, hidden them, perhaps never to be found again. But I'm looking. And hoping. Looking to whatever future is left for me, and hoping for the peace I believe I will find there.

I am becoming more free and feeling less and less inhibited and afraid. Although I had been placed in a position to take charge of both Dad and Mother and their household as well as my own, I never recognized my inner strength. The things I did, the decisions that needed to be made; I simply reacted and accomplished. I went through each day, one day at a time, not thinking of what my tomorrows would be like, not looking ahead and not considering myself and my own needs. There would be time for that later. Well, now is later and I feel I am arriving, at last, at my own party, ready to live my own life, my own way.

After Nancy's beating and her disappearance, I didn't ask about her. I was afraid to, since when Edda disappeared out of my life earlier, I had asked, "Where's Edda?" And Dad told me, "Your sister was bad, so she was taken away, and her clothes were taken off her, and she was put in a little cage, forever, like an animal." What a horrible thing to tell an impressionable little girl, and how very frightened I was, thinking, If Dad thinks I'm bad, I'll end up in a cage too. Nothing more was said or asked about Edda, therefore I didn't want to hear or know the same thing, or somewhat the same thing, about Nancy. She wasn't bad, she was good. She was beautiful. I didn't know the truth about Edda for many years to come. She had appeared in high school so often with black eyes and severe bruises that she was finally taken to the principal, who called in the town attorney, and they had removed her immediately to a foster home. I didn't know the truth about Nancy.

To this day, I'm claustrophobic. I can't sleep in a bed against a wall, or if I roll over and my hand or foot touches a wall I quickly awaken in a panic. Am I in a cage? And it takes me a few minutes to come back to my reality. This is life. Do I have my clothes on, I think? Where am I? Who am I? It does take me a few minutes to become aware of who I am and where I am. As a child, whenever I was bad I was put in the cellar into the darkness, not beaten, just horribly, horrifically frightened, and threatened. I wasn't tall enough to reach the light switch so I sat huddled on the step, in deep fear and dread, never knowing how long I'd be left there. Sometimes it was longer than other times—it didn't matter, it always seemed an eternity. It was at that time that I began to let go of my mind and be in a far more peaceful, beautiful place. I still cannot live in a house without at least a 40-watt bulb on somewhere, all night long. I was always afraid in that house I grew up in. Even after Mother and Dad had passed away, I'd never go into that house alone. I'd always ask Edda to meet me there, to help me clean out the house. Then came that day.

The door to the past began to open soon after Dad died, eight months after Mother had passed away. My sister Edda and I would meet at our parents' house to go through papers, and to try to sift through all the debris collected through the years. One Saturday I was leaning on the doorway to our parents' bedroom, and happened to look up, and saw, I believe for the first time, the padlock. I suddenly felt very sick to my stomach. The padlock was rusted with age, and had obviously been there a very long time. I mentioned it to my sister, and she said she'd seen it, and wondered if Dad has used it through the years to keep my demented and very alcoholic mother under control, though not in either of our memories. Trying to go through one of my mother's bureaus, I found a few old eight- or sixteen-millimeter films. They were pornographic. There were also pictures, sketches of men and women in various sexual positions. Edda and I tried to cover our disgust with a moment of levity, picturing our stiff old mother and our dad, who was built like a Buddha, in those impossible situations. Perhaps a couple of athletic types, but not Mother with Dad or any man, nor Dad with Mother or any other woman. It just wasn't physically possible—and there was the rubber penis. They were disgustingly sick, just as my mother had always been.

We moved to this house when I was about two years old. There was a brook that ran through the yard, and when I was about two-and-a-half we had gone swimming. I was always the tag-along to my sisters; one was four years older than I, one six years older, and they always went swimming, and I wanted to go swimming too. We had a dog, part Airedale and part God only knows what, but Pal was our pal; we were never anywhere that our Pal wasn't with us. We were swimming and I was paddling, and because my sisters always felt that I had been Mother's little treasure, so to speak, they encouraged me to go into the deep part of the brook. I went into the deep part, which was perhaps two feet deep, and was encouraged to swim across to them. Like a rock, I went down for the count. And the next thing I remember is hearing one of them say to the other, "Is she dead? I think she's dead. Mother will kill us." And I remember Pal licking my face as I lay on the bank burbling and gurgling and coughing and spitting and spewing. Pal had come into the water and pulled me out by the little pair of training pants that I had had on that summer day, and I was not dead. I had been saved. God sends angels in many forms, very often with four legs and scruffy red hair. That was my Pal.

It's my belief that at our birth, God blesses us with a soul, a spirit, and fills our hearts with his love (which we can increase or decrease depending on the pathway we choose), with free will, and certainly with guardian angels. The more we increase God's love, the more angels are sent to surround and protect us.

Another time when I was probably around three and a half years old, probably the following summer, my sisters decided to paint clothes on me. In those days, house paint was lead-based, and, once again in my training pants, I stood there, naive and gullible as always. Whatever my sisters did, I followed their lead: they were older, they were bigger—they were always right. And I stood there as they painted a little blouse on me, they painted a little skirt on me, they painted shoes and socks on me, they even put makeup on me with house paint. And then they sent me to my mother, who was drinking with the maid next door. I rang the doorbell, Mother answered the door, took one look at me, and went over in a dead faint. The next thing I remember was being stuck, placed, in the kitchen sink at our house, sitting in a few inches of kerosene with mother scrubbing the flesh off me, saying, "Your father's going to kill us all when he gets home, your father's going to kill us all." And that's how my mother cleaned me, scrubbing and scrubbing and scrubbing, with kerosene. I don't remember much about it, except that it really burned.

The maid was a lovely tiny little lady of African American descent, who, like my mother, enjoyed her afternoon break, not with coffee or tea, but with alcohol. She was the first black person I had ever encountered and I was really quite fond of her. I even today have a couple of her recipes, which I bake on occasion.

Another time my sisters thought it would kind of be their way of dispensing with me, so to speak. One of them told me they did try to get rid of me, the other one says they didn't really mean to kill me. The important thing is today we all love one another. Sibling rivalry doesn't exist any longer. We had a large maple tree in the back yard overlooking a bank. My dad had hung a swing there for my sisters and me. I wanted to swing too; whatever my sisters did I wanted to do. Taking turns on the swing, they would pump their legs, and by giving one another a hearty push would go so high, it to me seemed like flying into the sky. They always laughed and it just seemed like wondrous fun. They seemed free, like birds flying. So my sisters helped me onto the swing, which went over the bank, probably 12 feet or so, and said to me, "Carrie, you'll get a better ride if you hang on real low on the swing." So I moved my hands down the rope to the seat and hung on tight. As I did, they gave me a very healthy push and over I went, toppling and spinning and screaming, certainly not like a bird. I was swinging, all right, right into the sky and into a forever place. They finally caught me and pulled me off the swing. I thought I was going to die. My sisters were at first a bit frightened; I suppose they felt I was going to drop off and break my neck.

Another time, when children from the neighborhood were playing with them, they had climbed onto the garage roof, and I wanted to get up on the roof, too. Anything they did, I wanted to do. So they helped me up onto the garage roof, then after awhile I got bored, and said, "How do I get down?" They had been encouraged by the other children, knowing I'd want to follow. I guess I was quite an annoyance to the older kids, so they assumed if I were scared enough I wouldn't be such a tagalong. One of them handed me an umbrella. I don't know where it came from, but they handed me an umbrella, and I was told, "Just hold your nose with one hand, hold onto the opened umbrella with the other hand, and close your eyes and jump." That's exactly what I did—and went down like a rock, landing on my feet with a thump. Thank God, I was not hurt.

The maid next door, Janie, was a lovely lady, but she did drink. She would come down and drink with Mother in the afternoon and then go home and take her nap. The people she worked for had a pair of setter dogs, bird dogs. One of them was named Suzie. Suzie loved alcohol, almost as much as Mother and Janie did. When Mother would set her glass down in the grass outside in the yard, Suzie would meander over and lap until her tongue couldn't reach any deeper into the glass, and Mother would pick up her glass and say, "Oh! I must have drunk it all. I think I'll have another one. Would you like another one, Jane?" And Janie would say, "Yes, Mildred, I think I'll have another one too," and Mother would go into the house and come out with two more glasses of whiskey and whatever, and they would proceed to start drinking again. Soon Suzie would just kind of come over to me, lay her head on my lap, and go to sleep. My sisters were in school, and when the weather was nice, Mother and Janie sat outside on the lawn and I'd take my doll and sit a bit apart from them on the grass, not particularly mindful of their conversation or what was going on around me, except for the fact that Suzie always seemed thirsty. It was much later that I recognized that Suzie liked alcohol and always got tipsy. As she staggered up the hill following Janie, I guess I just thought, "She's still half asleep."

I wasn't aware until many years later that people who drink usually have a yen for the camaraderie of like people. This made Mother and Janie's association understandable.

After awhile, Janie would say, "Well, Mildred, I've got to go home, it's time for me to take my nap." And Mother would say, "I think I'll take a nap too." And Mother would go into the house, and that would leave me to my own resources.

When I was three or four, Mother and Dad had friends, Mary and Lester. Dad worked with Lester, and if memory serves me correctly, they had gone to grammar school together. Mary and Lester were building a house in another town and had nowhere to stay, so Mother and Dad let them stay with us. They slept on the sofa bed, and drank as much as Mother did, all day long. Sad to say, this was where the hard part begins.

My sisters would be sent up to bed before me, and I was kept downstairs. My sisters had brown hair and darker eyes than I. Mother always referred to me as her little Shirley Temple. Lester and Mary were childless, and Mary wanted to adopt me. She always spoke of taking me home with them when their house was ready for them to move in. It was after Edda and Nancy were sent up to bed, and Dad and Lester had gone out, probably to a bar, I don't know where, that Mother and Mary would take me into the bedroom, and that's where the oral sex began. Mother and Mary lay across the bed, and I can still hear Mother saying, "Do me first. Do me first." And I can still hear Mary saying, with a glass in her hand, "Do me next, do me next." I don't recall how it had all begun. I don't even recall how I had been directed to perform this disgusting duty on Mother and Mary, whether I was simply told "do this" and not knowing any other way, I did it. I only know that in the writing and remembering of this situation in my life, it still makes me want to cry. I still get nauseous and feel filthy. Poor reader, bear with me—I cannot go further into detail, only may God forgive them both!

After they were through with me, they would send me up to bed, where there wasn't any electricity, and I would find my way up to my bed, and I would lie, in a little fetal position, and cry and cry. I never told my sisters what went on. I never told anyone, until now, I am telling the world. My sister Nancy would get out of her bed and come to me in my bed, in that attic bedroom where the three of us slept, and she would cuddle me and put her arms around me, and say to me, "It's all right, Carrie, it's all right. It won't be long and we'll be grown up, and we'll be out of this house, and we'll never have to come back again. It's all right. You're all right now." We were all very young, and not as advanced in the ways of the world as children today at these ages might be. That's when I began wetting the bed. I was terrified to go downstairs to the bathroom, I was terrified to get out of my bed once I was safely in it.

That went on until I was probably four or four and a half years old, until I was really able to talk and carry on conversations. I became a very quiet withdrawn little girl, a very well-behaved little girl, one might say, doing as I was told. I listened to Mother scream, "Edda, you're not cooking that right!" She made my sister do the cooking, made my sister do the cleaning, made my sister do the laundry. Then one day, Edda was gone.

But before that happened, I had an accident with a baseball bat resulting in a skull fracture. It wasn't until many years later that I had the CAT scan, after the migraines and the periods of time when I wouldn't know what was going on, and I was finally diagnosed as having petit mal seizures, probably from that fracture. All of my face had been broken, especially on the right side. The good Dr. Rogel had remolded my face to look pretty much like my sisters. Never beautiful, like my sister Nancy, never beautiful like my sister Edda, but close enough so the family resemblance was there. My sister remembers that I was unconscious for four or five days, lying on the sofa. The doctor would come in and sit me up, force a little broth down my throat, and lay me back down, and clean me up. He did this every day, until one day I opened my eyes and he said, "I think she's going to be all right now." My sister Edda told me that she and Nancy would stand beside me looking down at me, and would call to me, and my eyes would flutter and try to open. But I didn't really respond, and I don't really remember it. I only remember that the afternoon when the doctor left after sitting me up and cleaning me off, my mother took me by the arm into the bathroom and, shoving my face in the bathroom mirror, said, "There. See how ugly you are? You'll never be pretty again. No one will ever want you. No man will ever want you."

I looked at the little face in the mirror, yellow and brown and swollen and discolored and purple, distorted, and a vision of that little face was with me for so many years, every time I would go to put makeup on, looking in the mirror, that little face would appear and I would think, "Little girl, I don't know who you are, but you're with God now, you're safe, you can leave." It wasn't until many years later that I realized the little face I was seeing was my own little face that afternoon, in that bathroom mirror, and my mother's words in my ears. Since I now am aware, I no longer see that little face, it's gone. It's just one more thing I had to encounter within myself, one more thing I had to face. It's only now, today, that I have mirrors in my home. Until now, I only had a bathroom mirror and a makeup mirror in my house. That little face would always catch me unaware.

Many years later, after I'd married and after the birth of my second child, I was visiting Mother and Dad while my husband was working, on a Sunday morning. Lester and Mary had long since moved into their house, which never was finished, and Lester came into Dad and Mother's house, and said, with a very strange look on his face, "Jesus Christ, Nick, there's something the matter with Mary. She hasn't moved in a couple of days. She won't even take a drink." My father and mother looked at each other and my father said, "I'll follow you home, Lester." And Dad went out, following Lester, and drove to his house. Mary was dead. When Dad came back to the house, he helped Lester make the arrangements, and I thought, how strange, I have no feeling, I have no feeling whatsoever. Mary is dead, and I just don't care. It's as though they were talking about someone I had never known. I had blocked her right out of my mind. I'd only seen her perhaps twice after they moved, and I put her out of my mind—like a nightmare.

Dad had a way of wanting me and my oldest sister to go to the wakes and funerals with him, not with my mother, and I thought, how very strange; he won't take his own wife to these things. He makes us go. So I had to go to Mary's wake. It was the first wake I had ever been to. I didn't know what was expected of me. I didn't know what they were like. As Dad and I walked in, Dad introduced me to people who evidently remembered me, but I didn't remember them, and we went to the coffin and Dad kneeled down, and I just stood there, and Dad tugged my hand, and I then kneeled, and I thought, what do you do now? But I didn't say anything, and soon we left. Dad said to me, "Why didn't you want to kneel?" and I said, "Dad, I've never been to a wake before, and I didn't know what it was like. I didn't know what was expected of me. I didn't realize I was suppose to kneel. What do you do when you kneel?" He said to me, "You're supposed to say a prayer." You must understand that as a Roman Catholic, when you're in church and you kneel, you pray. But this wasn't in a church; this was at a funeral parlor, and I didn't know what to do. I thought, oh, will God forgive me? I didn't say that prayer. But something inside of me really didn't care. Mary was gone, and I was relieved. It was over.

Going back to when I was a very young child, I very often wished I had been an adopted child, and my real parents would come and get me and rescue me from that house. How often I wished that. But it never happened, because the fact was, I was living with my real parents.

When I was very young, as I would meet people I would always raise my hand to shake theirs. I would know whether they were good people or whether they were not nice people, just by touching them. I would reach out and shake their hands, and the adults thought, "How very cute, how very dear, what a nice little girl, what a polite little girl." In later years, reading Carl Jung, I realized the feeling I got was their positive or negative energy fields, the vibration they emitted, The area which surrounds each of us—our own personal psyche-worlds!

In Carl Jung's book *Memories, Dreams, and Reflections*, he not only reflects on psychology and philosophy, but carries them into the spiritual. Jung had been a student of Sigmund Freud, but when he realized they had reached a point of diversity of opinions and theories and philosophies he left Freud and went on to his own heights. This book in particular was one I'd read in high school, and it left me with many great impressions as well as many questions, some of which are yet to be answered. But I feel I'm getting there, also. Now I realize that when I shake someone's hand, I can feel her energies; when I give her a kiss on the cheek I can feel her energies, and I know whether they're positive or negative energies, or a combination.

As a little girl I began to withdraw into myself, and live in my own kind of little world. I had a make-believe friend named Margie. I would play with my one doll, and Margie and I would play very quietly by ourselves, and I would chatter away with Margie. Mother would get so aggravated with me for talking to myself. She didn't realize I was talking to Margie. I couldn't actually see her, yet for me she was real and always there when I needed a playmate. Perhaps I was merely musing out loud, for I can't recall at any time her responding. Mostly I spoke of our doll babies and the clothes I'd make and how to dress and keep them clean. One afternoon, in the fall, I had been out in the yard, and the little brown and black caterpillars were out at that time of the year. I loved them, and I picked one up. You have to keep bouncing them, otherwise they'll start crawling. I had one in my sweater pocket, and of course I was bouncing my hand in my little sweater pocket, and I walked by my mother with my hands jammed in little fists in my sweater pocket. Always my hands were in my pockets when I walked past my mother, and I was always thinking, Please let me get past her without her noticing me. Please let me get past her without her noticing me. But I had this fuzzy caterpillar, and Mother was afraid of everything. Mother was simply terrified of anything and everything. As I bounced this little caterpillar up and down in my pocket, Mother reached out and grabbed my arm, demanding, "What are you doing in your pocket?" I let the caterpillar go in my pocket, held my hand out, and showed her an empty palm, and looked at her and said, "Nothing." My mother reached in my pocket, and when she did she pulled out the caterpillar. It was the second time in my life I saw my mother faint. And that time I thought it was really funny. I was a couple of years older then, and I thought that was funny. I was not yet in school, but I had begun to sense my power and capabilities over her.

We were born and grew up during the Depression, throughout the 30s, and it was difficult for a man to feed a family, and Dad had three children he was responsible for and had to feed. As I said, we lived in an attic bedroom. We would wake up in the morning—it was an unfinished attic bedroom—and a carcass would be hanging from the rafters: Daddy had killed another cow. We didn't realize our father had been out poaching deer. But Mother cooking it made it totally inedible. Mother's cooking was atrocious. Sometimes, when the weather was good, I would pass my food to my sister Nancy, who would scrape her dish into Edda's dish, and Edda, who sat next to a window in the little kitchen, would scrape all of it out the window, to our waiting dog Pal, who would gladly eat every bit of it. Poor Pal must have had a digestive system like a dinosaur. Anyway, somehow we survived. Somehow we survived not only Mother's cooking, but also Mother's brand of domesticity and punishments, and just being "Mother." As we were very young, Dad did much of the cooking and there was always Grams who would bring a meal to us. Grams, like a guardian angel, lived near enough to us to keep a close eye on us and look out for us. Yes. We survived, and rose above it all.

There were the awful mornings that my mother—I don't know if it was every family during those awful days, or if it was just my mother's way—but we were lined up every morning in front of that refrigerator, and the tablespoon and the cod liver oil came out, and one by one, we each got a tablespoon of cod liver oil. I can't tell you how awful that stuff tasted, and it never occurred to Mother to follow it with even a little sugar. Poor little Nancy, the cod liver oil would go down and Nancy would run right into the bathroom and it would come back up again. Edda and I had to stand there and swallow, and I can't tell you—sometimes when you're swallowing a tablespoon of cod liver oil, as a little child, you have to swallow three and four times before you can actually keep it down, and God only knows how long it takes before the taste and the smell get out of your mouth and your nose. Probably the only really good thing our mother ever did for us was to force us to take that cod liver oil. It was probably the one good thing she really did, because today we have strong bones and are healthy people. She was ordered by the doctor to give it to us, and it was Grams who, when she came to visit, would always check the bottle to see how much was gone and ask us if we were getting it each morning.

CHAPTER II

The War Years and the Cold War Years

"Give me your tired, your poor/your huddled masses yearning to breathe free/the wretched refuse of your teeming shore./Send these, the homeless, tempest-tost, to me./I lift my lamp beside the golden door."
From The New Colossus, by U.S. poet Emma Lazarus

Around the age of six was the time for me to begin first grade. I had already begun to read, and I was a very avid little reader; I was very well beyond my years in reading, and I seemed to comprehend whatever I did read. Although I enjoyed school, my report card, sad to say, always stated, "Carol is a very bright student, but she daydreams too much." Of course we didn't know about the petit mal seizures at that time. There were the usual childhood diseases: measles, mumps, and tonsillitis. Heaven forbid, there was constant tonsillitis, and good Dr. Rogel had to visit frequently. In those days when you had tonsillitis, your throat was "painted" (as it was called) with iodine. I have to tell you, that is almost as bad as cod liver oil. Twice a day Dr. Rogel would come in and paint my throat with iodine, and eventually the tonsillitis would go. This went on until I was probably eight or nine years old, when I had my tonsils removed.

But in the meantime, school had begun, and suddenly there was a war, World War II. It was rather meaningless at first to me, until things began to happen, strange things. Shades needed to be bought for the house, window shades, black ones. There was a period, night after night after night, in the winter, when we were not allowed to light anything but a little candle. We were allowed to listen to the radio, and Gabriel Heater, who came on every night, always stated, "There's bad news tonight." He would report the news as it was happening in the South Pacific and, a bit later, in Europe. It was a very sad time. There were ration stamps. Food was rationed. School was carried over, and we went on Saturdays as well, because most parents were either in the military, called into the draft, or working for the war effort in the factories. In my case, my dad worked in a factory; he was too old to be drafted, although he tried to join, I believe mostly to get away from Mother, but nevertheless, he did try to join. Because he had no sons to carry on the family name, they would not take him, but he was 39 years old at the time, and they were drafting men 39 years old. Dad was stung by the rejection. He got a job in a foundry in a nearby city which kept him away from home day and night and he only came home either for a party with his military buddies, or on a Sunday, now and then, to make us a good meal. Dad was a good cook, and we always hoped he would come home—at least to cook.

A lovely lady neighbor, who owned the dog Suzie, taught me how to knit. Mrs. Secam did not simply teach me how to knit with two needles. When Mrs. Secam taught you something, she taught you, and my mind was like a sponge, and I was willing to learn. She taught me with four needles. She taught me how to knit mittens with one finger and a thumb, and she taught me how to knit socks, and how to turn a heel. I realize today how difficult that sort of thing is, and how many people cannot do it. But she taught me, because she was head of the Red Cross. Red Cross didn't mean anything to me, except for the fact that the Red Cross collected things for our fighting men. I was just beginning my religious classes at that time, and I was just beginning to learn about God, and as I would knit with my four little needles, those mittens and those socks for the soldiers, one at a time, in that ugly olive drab color, I would think, dear God, please may he come home safe. Please may he come home safe. I'm certain there were many stitches that were dropped, but I don't think whoever got my socks and my mittens cared about a dropped stitch. They had dry socks and dry mittens in those foxholes in Europe when they were needed. One sock, one mitten at a time. Size didn't matter.

But the one finger kind of troubled me; I didn't understand it, and I asked Mrs. Secam, "Why do we not make mittens like my mittens that have all of the fingers together?" And she explained to me, they had to have their trigger finger free. Dad was a hunter, so I understood guns, and I understood a trigger finger. That meant somebody was dying. And to me, something dying meant that an animal was dying. That's the way it was with Dad, that's the way I grew up, that's the way I was growing up, that's the way I lived. Something was dying. It wasn't until I began to read the newspapers, and the newspaper accounts of the war, that I realized that it wasn't a thing that was dying, it was people that were dying, and some of those people were Americans. And I became patriotic. I really became patriotic, and am to this day. This is my country, and I'm awfully proud of it.

So I did the knitting, and I did my job, my duty for my country, as a little six- seven- and eight-year-old girl. That was my job, and Mrs. Secam saw to it that my job got done, God bless her. I read the newspaper accounts and the war proceeded, and I read of the Jews, and the Christians, and the gypsies, and people in the camps, but it wasn't until after the war, when the reports and the pictures in the newspapers were being published, and I began to see the death camps, that I began to realize what was happening to these people, and why it was so important for us to be in Europe, a place that I couldn't even locate on the map. It was so far removed, so very far removed from my world, and yet so very close, brought close by the darkness at night, brought close by the stamps that had to be collected to buy tanks. We had to collect our savings stamps. They were ten cents a piece, and when we filled a book it would buy a bond, a savings bond, a war bond, and when our school class had collected enough bonds—we were one of those beautiful little schools, two rooms; eight grades and two rooms—we bought a tank, and that tank meant some of our young men were going to come home alive, and free again, and we too would be free, and the airplanes would fly over our little world, and fly over, and fly over, incessantly, going toward Europe, coming back from Europe. In those days it seemed they flew quite low and when we would hear one coming during daylight hours, we would run out and wave to them.

Dad had several friends who had been called to the military, childless friends; some were not married, some were married, but they were childless. Some came back, some never came back. Then I began to really realize, between the pictures of the camps and the men who didn't come back, what war was really about. Having food rations, not having sugar, not having even the barest necessities, was what the war was like to me, but I began to realize what the war was really like to the people where the war was being waged.

After the war, there were people who were referred to as D.P.s, displaced persons. I didn't understand the phrase D.P. at the time, but I was in school, and suddenly a little boy named Dimitri appeared at school one day. He spoke no English. He wore his hair in a very peculiar style, and the other children made fun of him. They bullied him, they teased him. He was perhaps 10 or 11 years old, but he was really very small for his years. He had lived through the war, and as a displaced person had been brought to this country, to freedom, to this great country, and a family had taken him in. I was asked to teach him to read, the first year primer, "run Spot run, see Dick run, see Jane run," to help him learn English. He knew he was being made fun of, and he would fight back the tears, just as I'm sure he fought back the tears when his family was taken from him. One day Dimitri was gone, they moved him out of my school; they moved out of town, and I rather missed him. I had befriended him. He needed a friend and I needed to befriend someone. He needed to know that somebody loved him, and I really cared for him. A little girl caring for a little boy, both of us having lived through our own private wars.

Time went on, and the war was over, finally, and men came back. Men without legs, men without arms, men without eyes. It was a terrible time, and yet it was a great time, because we were once again at peace. Yet we weren't at peace; we were beginning to get into the Cold War—General Patton had said, "Let's fight those Communists, let's get them now while they're weakened." And our president had said, "I will be the judge of that." And we didn't do it, and the Cold War began. And in the Pacific area, Gen. Douglas MacArthur said "Let's fight those Communists, let's fight the Chinese back, and keep them out of the way."

There was Hiroshima. I remember reading the book *Hiroshima* by John Hersey; it was the first edition of the book; I'm not sure you could even get it today. The pictures of what the atom bomb did were horrible. I'm certain the men of the *Enola Gay* had no idea what was going to happen. But they did their duty. They were in uniform, they were given orders, and they obeyed their orders, and they dropped their bombs. Hiroshima and Nagasaki were obliterated, and children like me were lost in the devastation.

There was the Potsdam Conference, between Churchill, Roosevelt and Stalin, deciding what to do with the few remaining Jews who were left in Europe. Stalin wanted them to go to Yugoslavia, a piece of Yugoslavia. Something inside of me said, please dear God, please dear God, let this not be, let them go to Palestine. Let them go home. Please dear God. I instinctively knew, if they were allowed or sent to Yugoslavia, Stalin would finish the pogrom that Hitler had begun, that had begun originally in Russia. They would have been totally gone, en masse. This must not be.

Thank God, they were allowed to go to Palestine, and David Ben Gurion, one of the greatest heroes of the century, led his people to build a country, a beautiful country, out of a piece of desert rock, a mosquito-infested, malaria-infested, area. He led his people to freedom. He fought against the English, who said, "No, I don't want them here," but he held his ground, and now we have the state of Israel. Thank you, God. The Jews are home, where they belong.

At about the same time, there were the Nuremberg Trials, the trials for the remaining Nazis—the general who oversaw the war against the Jews, the Christian, the gypsies. Thank God for the wisdom of the judges in charge of the Nuremberg trials, the Nazis were dispensed with, one by one by one. So therefore, the war was over.

In the meantime, I made my first Holy Communion. There were only three of us in my Communion class, and that's when I received my rosary beads, which I carry with me today. To this day I carry those rosary beads, given to me by the Church, when I made first Holy Communion in first grade. Those poor little rosary beads have seen so many prayers, for so many people, and I thank God, the Church gave me my greatest treasures of all, my rosary beads. And yet today, I also wear a Star of David, because sometimes I don't know whether I am, in my heart, more Jewish than I am Roman Catholic Italian. But it doesn't matter. God knows, and God knows I believe. I believe so intensely, so strongly, and God knows I go to Him daily, I talk to Him daily, I communicate with Him daily, and God is with me, as he always has been. Many of the displaced persons who were brought to this country, I am sure, thank the same God that I thank, for opening our doors to our people, because that's what this country was based on. That's why it was always called the melting pot of the world. People from all over the world have always been welcomed to this country.

By the time I was ten, I was supposed to have made confirmation, which I didn't make until long after my divorce, when my daughter made hers. It seemed the right time, the time to become fully sacramented with the one child of mine whom I'd always looked upon as my legacy. Mother was in her usual alcoholic condition, and Nancy and I did not make confirmation the year we were supposed to, because Mother had had an argument with the Church. Whether or not Nancy made it later I don't know, but I do know that I eventually did make it. At any rate, we continued to go to church, and life went on. After the war, playtime, whatever time there was left for playing, again began, and I wanted to join the older kids playing. We would go next door, to the old house and the old barn, and we would play hide-and-go-seek, and of course I was always the one that was "it." On the rare occasions when I was allowed not to be "it," I would scurry up to the barn where the hay was kept and I would reach into the hay and feel around with my little hands until I found the mouse nest. I always was able to find a little mouse nest, and I would very carefully take the little mice in my hands, and I would talk to them, carefully press them against my cheek, and then I would very carefully put them back in their little nest. I wasn't afraid of them, and I wasn't afraid of the dark in that barn. The only place I was afraid of the dark was at home.

I suppose I've known many little helpless "mice" during my lifetime. People I've loved, people I've been able to help in one way or another. And there were those times when I was the little mouse being helped by others who were kind, compassionate, and loving. I recall rather recently, approaching the steps to a restaurant. Ahead of me was a thirtyish woman accompanied by a much older woman using a walker. They got to the steps and the younger woman simply went on ahead, not ever holding the door for the older woman, who I supposed was her grandmother. The older woman looked around, saw me, and suggested I go on ahead also. I said, "No, I'll just rest my hand on your back and follow behind you. I have plenty of time." The older woman smiled and looking at my smaller frame said, "If I slip and fall backward, I'll crush us both!" I laughed and motioned her on, knowing neither of us would fall. There would be no accident. And of course there wasn't. It only took a few extra moments of my time, but the smile of gratitude from her when we reached the door added years to my life and made my day—perhaps it made her day, also. And very often I was the little mouse, helped by another such as Mrs. Secam, Dr. Rogel, Grams, Grandfather—the list goes on and on, continuing with my mentor who guided me in the writing of this book, and Dr. K., among those who encouraged me to write it.

Going back to the beginning of the little town I was raised in: it was part of what was called Humphreysville. It included several towns which broke away eventually, and the house that I was just referring to, where the barn was, had been an inn, and during the Revolutionary War people would go there and their horses and carriages were stabled in this barn. I didn't mind going into this house, it didn't bother me at all, I liked it; as a matter of fact I loved this house. I loved being in the attic. There was something very comfortable and cozy about it. There wasn't electricity, but I didn't mind that, but there was something very comfortable about being in the attic. But I could never bring myself to go alone into the basement.

Someone had to go with me. I later learned that there were underground tunnels from this basement, where our Revolutionary soldiers would rest, or would escape the British, and some of them had died there. I just felt very uncomfortable going down there. Perhaps some people might say, Oh well, I suppose she felt the ghosts of the soldiers who died there. I don't know what it was; I just didn't feel comfortable going into the cellar of that house. And I could never live in that house, knowing what had gone on in the basement. But other than that, I loved the house. I loved the house, the second floor, and the attic. And I loved the barn.

I've never seen a ghost, but the older kids used to tease me about them. At that age I didn't know what a ghost was. It wasn't until a few years later while reading a poem in which the word "spectre" was used and looking it up in the dictionary and rereading that part of the poem, I knew and learned about them. I think what I felt in the cellar of that old house were the lasting impressions one leaves behind, our atmosphere which trails behind us when leaving the presence of another—our "energies." It's like walking into someone else's home and feeling a tension, and yet in another person's home you feel quite peaceful and comfortable. That's the sort of sense I'm attempting to describe.

Time went on. As I mentioned, I was a very avid reader. I was reading very much beyond my years, and Dad had decided to buy a set of encyclopedias. I enjoyed those encyclopedias, I was able to visualize what I was reading, and being able to visualize was something I simply assumed everyone and anyone could do, but being without my older sister, and with my second sister being so much older than I and at an age when she was reluctant to have me hanging off her—loving me but not needing me around—I would lose myself in my books. I would read and be a part of what I was reading. I can do that to this day; it matters not what kind of a book I read. The books I read are historical, are religious, are spiritual. I don't waste my time reading trashy books. I don't waste my time doing such things. If there had to be one room for me to be locked away in for the rest of my life, I pray it would be a library room.

During the years I was going to grammar school after the war, Mother's girlfriend Mary had decided to raise Pomeranians, and of course whatever Mary did Mother had to do too, so Mother had to get her Pomeranians, and had gotten a little black one called Curly. Curly and I were good buddies. I came from school one day, it was icing, the weather was just terrible, and Mother was really being brutal to this little tiny dog, she was spanking him and screaming at him, for whatever breach Heaven knows. I saw what

Mother was doing to Curly. Outside in our driveway we had a little maple tree, kind of a boundary-line tree, which is still there. I quickly put my mittens and my coat on, took the little dog, put him in my coat, and climbed the tree. I knew we would be safe in that tree. I sat there, freezing, with the dog, trying to keep him warm and keep him from Mother. I waited until Dad came home. I don't know how much time had gone by. Dad finally came home and went into the house. I was too cold to call to him. I was frozen. My coat was frozen on me, my mittens were frozen on me. I was too cold to call out to him, Dad, help me. Dad came out of the house and started calling me. "Carrie, where are you, Carrie, where are you?" I finally answered, "Dad, I'm up here." He came to the tree and he said, "Carrie, what the hell are you doing up in the tree?" And I called down to him, "Dad, I had to get Curly, I had to save Curly, Mother was going to kill him. I had to save Curly." And Dad helped me down out of the tree. Helped me into the house. He said to me, "Get those things off, take your clothes off immediately, and get your pyjamas on. Get into some warm, dry clothes." And he took Curly out of my arms. By this time Mother was unconscious in the bedroom, and I looked at him and I said, "Dad, don't let her hurt him. Please don't let her hurt him." He said, "Don't worry about it, she's sleeping for the night, she won't hurt anybody now." And I said, "Dad, can I take Curly upstairs with me?" He looked at me and said, "You poor little shit, get your pyjamas on, get warm, and get upstairs, I'll let you have the dog." As I explained earlier, the upstairs was an attic, with no insulation. It was cold, and in order to keep warm we had rocks that we kept in the oven, and those warm rocks we would take upstairs, put in our beds, to keep our feet warm, because if we kept our feet warm our bodies would be warm. So I got my pyjamas on, picked up my rock out of the oven, without having had any dinner to eat, picked up the little dog, and we went upstairs and we went to bed.

And so it went. There was always something Mother was going to do to someone, somewhere or somehow.

During the war years, getting back to the war years, there was my grandmother. My grandmother had seven children, all grown and married by this time. For some reason and somehow, my grandmother always managed to bring meat to the house. She would go to the store and buy a quarter of a beef, and she would go to each one of her daughters' houses and leave a portion of meat, so we would have meat. Where she got the money, I don't know. Grandmother was always concerned with her grandchildren, especially the three of us little girls, because my grandmother, my mother's mother, my Grams, knew. My mother had had two abortions, my grandmother knew that. My mother drank, my grandmother knew that. My mother was abusive, my grandmother knew that. My grandmother sheltered us whenever she could, she fed us whenever she could, she taught us how to cook whenever she could. She was a beautiful woman and I loved her until the day she died; I loved her dearly. She was my friend. As a little girl, when I was old enough, I would go through the woods to her house. Going through the woods in those days was a safe thing to do. We didn't have to worry about perverts, and we didn't have to worry about child kidnappers. There was nothing to worry about, it was a safe thing. You could walk through the woods to grandmother's house, as the poem says, and grandmother always welcomed us. Always. We loved to be there, and occasionally we were allowed to sleep overnight, and Grams always had her feather beds. She had her chamber pots, because she did not have indoor plumbing, and she had her lamps, oil lamps, because she did not have electricity either. But she had feather beds, and curling up into one of my grandmother's feather beds was one of the greatest joys of my childhood, and letting that bed sink around me and envelop me and fold over me—it was the most caressing, loving thing in my life during those days. I felt peace. I felt, I really felt loved, and I was loved, my grandmother loved me, and I was welcomed.

My other grandmother, my father's mother, was typically Italian. She spoke little or no English. Grandfather loved us dearly. Grandmother loved us, but she didn't know how to communicate with us. But I remember Grandmother always praying. Occasionally we were fortunate enough to go to the farm that Grandmother and Grandfather had, in another town, and going to that town on a Sunday was a real treat, because that meant I could run down to the barn when Grandfather was milking the cows, and as Grandfather would take the teats of the cow and spray for the cats who lived in the barn, he would also spray into a cup, a little tin cup that was always sitting there, and he would spray the milk from the cows, the warm delicious milk, straight from the cows into the cup, and nothing tasted better than the taste of that warm sweet milk, fresh from the cows, and the cow would turn around and give a little moo, as though it knew that I was being nourished. It was a form of love, and I loved it. I would pet the cow, and I would rest my head against her big old head. It was as though I was thanking her because I was grateful. The cats were grateful and happy and I was grateful and happy. They were good days. Those were good moments in my life and I enjoyed every bit of it.

But Grandmother did not approve of having animals in the house. There was a little dog, similar to a border collie, named Pennies, and when Grandmother knew that my father's kid sister, who was my godmother, and I had squirreled that little dog Pennies into the house, behind the old wood stove, Grandmother would get the broom, and out the door old Pennies would go. It didn't matter what the weather was, old Pennies had to get out of the house, because Grandmother said it was bad luck. The old Italian ways were with her until the day she died, and it was bad luck to have an animal in the house. Grandmother did not like my mother. Maybe my grandmother knew, I don't know. My grandmother knew very much and many things, without ever having had to be told. She knew. That knowing, that intuition, that link with God, was passed to my father, to me, to my children, we all have that link with God, that intuition, that spark. We all have it. That is the spark that I go back to when I was a little girl and knew what a person would be like by shaking their hands.

Of course we three children weren't aware of what made a "good life" from a "not-so-good life." We simply existed and lived each day and its experiences as they came. We knew that the visits with either set of grandparents would be happy—cousins and aunts and uncles to visit with and always good food and plenty of love, and we were always sad to see those delightful occasions end. There were the Italian meals, a real treat, at Dad's parents' home. The homemade ravioli and spaghetti, the homemade sauces, the Italian cookies—and the farm animals. And at Mother's parents' home, the cooking was always delightful and always plenty of it, also visits with cousins, aunts and uncles, and fun. Grandfather, who was Grams's third husband, was not a well man, but he was most tolerant of us little scamps. He allowed us to play in the barn, jumping from the hay loft into the soft hay below, and asking us to call the cows in for him at night. And Grams showing us how to churn the butter, which once started had to be continued always in the same direction or it would become lappered. I never knew what that meant, only that it meant the cream wouldn't become butter. There was always milk for us to drink and butter on the homemade bread. After Grandfather passed away, Grams continued to keep a watchful eye on her grandchildren, sometimes you could feel you belonged to her. She always had something for us to do to keep us occupied: jigsaw puzzles to be worked, the player piano she allowed us to play. Grams was a very generous, giving woman. I loved her then, and though she's been gone nearly forty years, I continue to miss her and love her.

Certainly life wasn't all darkness and shadows, there were occasional lighter times. I recall the night my sister and I awoke to some terribly loud yelling and caterwauling. Not aware of what was happening, we shushed each other and crept down the dark stairs of the attic and opened the door to hear Dad yelling, "Get out of the way, Mildred, I'm going to kill those goddamned cats." Suddenly we heard the shot of the rifle and the house went dark. The next minute Dad called out, "Jesus Christ, Mildred, I think I'm dead!" Mother answered, "I think you're okay, Nick. But the lights are out." We had a female cat which must have been "in season" and Dad, when he built the house, had never bothered to put in the glass window frames in the cellar; therefore, a tom cat must have gotten in and a bit of mating had been going on. When Dad fired at the cats, he also shot the BX cable in two, cutting off the power to the house. We quietly crept back upstairs and one of us whispered through our giggles, "Too bad it wasn't her," and back to sleep we went. All was well.

That was the same cat that I would dress up in my dolls' clothes, put into my doll carriage, and push around. She was such a dear patient little three-legged creature. Dad had brought her home when she was a kitten because she had been in some kind of accident and had lost one of her hind legs. She tolerated the lipstick I'd put on her and the nail polish on her front claws. She was such a good little "kittie." We had her for a few years, during which time there would be talk of her having kittens. I can't recall but once actually seeing a kitten or two, but when I got up the following day they were gone and nothing more was ever mentioned of them. I guess, as an adult today, there was little if any respect for life as I have grown to know it.

And of course, there was the baby opossum. Dad as I've mentioned was a "coon" hunter. One night, after my sisters were gone and I was alone with Mother and Dad, he came home, and as was my custom, I was waiting for him. He tied the dogs, fed them, and came in as I sat at the table finishing my homework. He had a silly grin on his face and asked, "Is your mother in bed?" I nodded yes and he came to me and held open his hunting jacket pocket saying, "Carefully reach in and take it out." I cautiously reached into his pocket and brought forth this little tiny baby opossum. Looking at Dad I asked, "Can we keep it?" Dad explained that the dogs had treed the mother; opossums are nocturnal, and the female always carries her litter clinging to her back when she's out feeding or whatever, and the dogs got her and Dad was able to rescue this one little baby. He said, "You know your mother will have a fit, but I guess it's okay until it's old enough to take care of itself."

We kept it for a couple of years. I'd get home from school and take it out of its box and carry it either in my pocket or in my arms. It knew it had nothing to fear from Dad or me and as it slept during daylight hours Mother either pretended it wasn't there or wasn't fully aware it was there. One night when it was a couple of years old, I awoke to Mother's screams, "Nick, that dirty thing is going to eat the door down!" I went downstairs and picked up "our" baby and, trying to calm Mother, Dad said, "Carrie, we've got to take it back to the woods. It's old enough to find a mate and we've got to let it go." It had lived behind the oil stove in the kitchen in a wooden box since it had arrived, and what Dad and I didn't realize was that it had chewed at the baseboard behind the stove and was working its way at night down the hall toward Mother and Dad's bedroom. It really had done quite a bit of damage and probably would have continued onward if its gnawing hadn't awakened Mother that night, and she, out of fear of it, was raving and frightening the poor little thing. The following Saturday evening, Dad and I reluctantly took it into the woods and I kissed it and we freed it. It was sad for me, but as Dad said, "It's nature's way."

And I go back to my little Curly. How I loved that little dog. He was missing one afternoon when I came home from school and I asked Mother where he was. Mother said, "I don't know, I haven't seen him all afternoon." It was cold, and once again it was snowing and there was ice. I went outside and I called and called, and, it seemed such a distance away, I heard little Curly barking back to me. That same little brook that I learned how to swim, or sink, in, whichever you wish, that same brook, a little farther up, Curly was stuck on a rock. His little toenails couldn't grasp the icy rocks and make it across. I don't know what he was doing there, probably getting away from my mother again, but he was stuck. I waded into that cold icy brook, picked him up, and brought him home. His hair was stiff with ice and snow, and he was cold. I don't know, I guess God had his hand on that dog, just like he had always had his hand on me. I brought Curly back into the house, took him to the oven door, and I took an old rag and I scrubbed him off and I got him toasty warm, and then I changed my own clothes and Curly and I once again went to bed.

The final thing about little Curly was when I had to have my tonsils out—I had tonsillitis for the final time and the doctor said, "This is it, she's got to have her tonsils out. They're so badly swollen they're almost closing her throat over. Her tonsils and adenoids have to come out." So off to the hospital I went, and I thought all night long after that surgery I could hear the click of his toenails coming down the hall, and I kept thinking, "They're bringing him." I didn't care whether or not I saw my mother and father, I just wanted to see Curly. I thought, I can hear him, I can hear him! They'll be coming through the door any minute. I can hear him, I can hear him. I could hear his little toenails. Later Dad said to me that Curly didn't sleep the night I was in the hospital. He ran back and forth all through the house. I gather Curly was looking for me just as I was looking for him. There really is a link between humans and dogs, especially children and dogs. Curly and I loved each other, but to Mother, Curly was simply a possession.

During these years, my sisters were gone, and I became Dad's son, so to speak. I was the one who went fishing with him, I was the one who went hunting with him, I was the one he took when he went just about everywhere. Dad didn't seem to have enough money for the necessities of life, but he always had enough money to order his hound dogs. Dad was a raccoon hunter, and this was the one sport he enjoyed. Any drinking or gambling he had done years before had ceased; he was now a hunter. Dad would order his dogs from Kentucky, Tennessee, Indiana. It would take a week, ten days, sometimes two weeks for his dogs to arrive, and they would be without water. They would come in a cage and they would be without water, or food, all the while they were traveling, unless, God willing, St. Francis willing, unless someone somewhere along the way would fill the little tin cup that was wired to the side of their cage. Dad would get the notice in the mail, "Your dog has arrived," and he would go down after work and pick up the dog. The rule of the house was, when Dad got a new dog, that night Dad would take the dog out, but the dog was not allowed to be fed first. Dad would bring the cage home, and I would sit and wait for Dad to come home, with a cup of water. I was allowed to give the dog the water, but I was not allowed to feed it. Hunting dogs were Dad's priority, and Dad's word was law. But I was allowed to give them water. Dad would take the dogs out the first night they arrived, hungry, and he would test them out. That was the one night that I was not wanted, and not asked to go hunting with him. Sometimes the dogs didn't come back and his comment was, "Jesus Christ, the goddamn dog wasn't any good. I left it in the woods." What he had done was, he would put the dog out of its misery and leave the carcass in the woods.

Anyway, one night a dog came. This dog had walker in it, it had collie in it—it was not a hunting dog. She just wasn't a hunting dog. I took a look at Lady Dog, and I said, "Dad, can I go with you tonight?" I didn't want her to be left in the woods. I gave her water. I gave her a second cup of water, she was so thirsty. She was a big dog, and long-haired, and red and white; she was a beauty, and I loved her immediately. Dad said, "No, you know what the rule is, you can't go out with me tonight." I begged and I pleaded and begged and pleaded, "Dad, please let me come with you tonight, please let me come with you tonight." He finally, condescendingly, said to me, "Oh, hell, you can come tonight." So off we went to the woods, and he opened the cage and turned Lady Dog loose, and he said to me, "Jesus Christ, Carrie, she must be a silent hunter, I don't hear her anywhere. We'll sit down and we'll wait until she trees a 'coon. Then we'll go find her." And we waited. And we waited. And we waited. A few hours had gone by, and he said, "Oh hell, Carrie, I'll just call her. She'll come. She's hungry enough, she'll come back." So we called her, and then he turned his big five-cell flashlight on, and she was standing behind us where we were sitting on the log, wagging her tail, and I put my arms around her, and I said, "Dad, can't we bring her in the house? Please can't we bring her in the house? Can't I keep her?" And Dad said, "Goddamn it, no, she's a hunting dog, she's gotta be tied out with the other hunting dogs." I said no more. We brought her home, Dad had her food all soaked and ready for her to eat, and while he was tying her up, I carried her pan of food down to her, and he said to me, "What the hell are you doing here?" And I looked at him and I said, "Dad, I want her in the house. I want her with me." And he said, "Goddamn it, no, Carrie, she's a hound dog. She's gotta stay out here." He took the pan of food from me, and handed it to her, and she ate. She was so hungry.

Well, we went out the next night, and we went out the third night. The fourth night there was no barking and my father said, "Goddamn it, Carrie, there's something wrong." He said, "I know there's something wrong. This goddamn dog isn't any good." I looked at him, in the dark, and I put my hand on his, and I said, "Dad, please, can't I keep her?" He said, "Your mother will kill us if I let you bring her in the house. She's too big." And I said, "Please Dad, please, Dad, call her and bring her back, and let me keep her." Well, he called her, he put the five-cell flashlight on, and there she was, curled in a ball, not two or three feet behind us. She never hunted, in the three or four days we had gone out with her. She was not a hunting dog. Dad picked up his rifle and went to aim it at her. I fell on her, and said, "Please, Daddy, please, Daddy, don't kill her! Don't kill her. Let me keep her!" And Dad said, "Oh, hell, Carrie, if you want the goddamn fool you can have her. But your mother's going to be awfully mad at all of us."

And I had my Lady Dog. My Lady Dog came into the house, and I fed her, and when I opened the door to go upstairs, my Lady Dog went up, and she seemed to know which bed was mine, and she got on my bed first, and I found my way to my bed and she was already on it, waiting for me. That was my Lady Dog. Every day she walked me out the door and sat on the edge of the lawn when I got on the school bus to go to school, and every afternoon she would be sitting on the edge of the lawn waiting for me to come home. That went on for a number of years, until one day the school bus driver, who was always teasing me about my dog waiting for me, saw that Lady Dog wasn't sitting on the lawn. The night before she couldn't make it up the stairs. I knew she was getting old, and I slept down on the sofa, and Lady Dog lay on the floor next to the sofa. Dad got up in the morning and he said to me, "What the hell are you doing down here?" I said to him, "Lady couldn't make it upstairs, Dad, and I didn't want to leave her alone." He just looked at me. I looked at Lady and I pet her and I scratched her and I gave her a kiss, and she walked me out to the bus that morning, but when I got home from school that afternoon she wasn't there. As with my sisters, I knew better than to ask. Lady Dog couldn't make it up the stairs, so Lady Dog was no more. Lady Dog was never mentioned again. The school bus driver said that day, teasing me, "Looks like your old dog is too lazy to come out today." He said it kind of teasingly, but I knew in my heart, I knew, I knew. My Lady Dog was gone.

Perhaps Lady Dog was the reason I am so attracted to my collies today. There's always been some kind of a dog in my life, and there always will be. Believe me, when you learn how to love a dog, and a dog has become your friend, and sometimes the only friend you have, it's awfully hard to give them up. I don't know where Lady Dog is, except I know her soul is with God, and she's at peace. But I have a feeling I've seen her in other dogs I've had since then, and I will always love her, just as I will always love my Curly. I will always love her. Through the years I have always had a dog with me, sometimes as many as three or four, but the most special ones of note would be my Angus, when the children were young, my daughters, and then my Blue Girl; she lasted one month short of her twentieth year. My Bupper, my last collie, and today, my Walker. They have each had that special something about them which told me how "knowing," or "intuitive" they were—are. My Bupper's ashes are in a canister with his collar on my bureau, as will be my Walker's, should be go before me, and those ashes will be buried with me along with my rosary beads and my Bible. Each were devoted, trusting, trustworthy, protective, and all giving and loving. It makes me wonder if dogs reincarnate, as I believe we do!

The work routine around the house had fallen on my shoulders. I was the one who now had to do the cooking, the cleaning, the laundry—which I did. One day it was time for me to graduate from grammar school, which I did, and I was in high school. I hated high school. I was ostracized, I was ridiculed. I thought it was because I was ugly; I had no idea it was because the whole town knew of the history of what went on in that house. I didn't know that, because I didn't know—I was too young to understand. I ran away from home three times, I went to New York. I don't know what a little girl of 14 thought she could do in New York, but I wanted to get far away, and I had nowhere to go. Three times God brought me back, and I thought my father would kill me, but he had been told, as my grandmother had explained to me, by the police and by the town council, after Nancy, when Nancy was brought to the foster home, "Nick, you have one more daughter, if she shows up with so much as a scratch on her, you and your wife will go to jail. And you'll never see your daughters again." I didn't know that, but the whole town did. So school was hell. As a freshman I had a teacher who no matter what I did, no matter what I wore, always gave me a slap on the ass when I walked through the door, and I would try to put someone between him and me because he stood at the door as we walked through the door to our classrooms. I hated it. I absolutely hated it. I dreaded going into that history class. And I didn't do well in that history class, though I do know my history and I enjoy history. But he made it hell for me. There were no laws on sexual harassment in those days, and to whom could I complain? I was basically shy and introverted.

I got through, and I met a few people, but I didn't date. I didn't make very many friends. It was a Polish town and I was an Italian, and although my grandparents came to this country with papers, I was considered a wop, so I know what it's like to have prejudices against you. I recall joining the CYO and going to a meeting one night and the priest made a comment about there being no other religions, and my mind went back to the Second World War and the Jews, and I said to him, "But Father, what about the Jews?" And he ordered me out of the church, never to return again. "There is no other religion but the Roman Catholic religion," he said. And I went home crying, humiliated. I can't really explain, but I was not even accepted at church. I was not accepted at school, I was not accepted at church. I simply was not accepted.

And I certainly wasn't accepted at home. I remember when I got my period for the first time. Nancy was still at home. I didn't know, because Mother wasn't the kind of mother to talk to any of us about things like that, and I went to her, and I said to her, "Mother, there's something wrong with me," and I showed her my pyjamas. She called me a filthy pig and threw a rag at me. It was really a rag. She said, "Put this on." I didn't know what she meant; I didn't know what was going on. My sister Nancy didn't know what was going on. She was late in beginning her menstruation; I was early. Nancy didn't know. I went to the lady next door, Mrs. Secam again, and I asked her about it. "What's wrong with me? Why does my mother think I'm a pig? What did I do wrong?" I just didn't understand. She explained the whole thing to me, and she explained that I now must be very careful and not let boys get near me, because that's how babies come about. She was very kind and gentle, and she was a beautiful woman, a really beautiful woman, and explained to me, I wasn't a pig; it was a natural thing but it was a very unusual age for me to begin becoming a woman. Things began to change at home. My mother treated me like I was dirtier than the rag she threw at me. She made me wash her rags. She did not buy the usual sanitary napkins that ordinary girls were wearing, she wanted me to wear rags. I had very heavy menstruations, and if it wasn't for this beautiful lady next door I would have had to go to high school wearing rags. But she kept me supplied with sanitary napkins and explained to me how to wear them, that this would happen once a month and I was to expect it, and if I was in any kind of discomfort I was to come to her and she would help me. Well, I had no discomfort; it wasn't until after my first baby was born that I knew what discomfort was, when I was menstruating.

I definitely handled my own daughter and her sexuality quite differently. We often talked and she would question me, and hopefully I directed the correct answer to her. This was a natural thing and a beautiful thing, which if you were blessed and lucky would develop into becoming a mother. My daughter had natural mothering, nesting instincts. She took under her wing a smaller little girl from the neighborhood and would go on picnics with her, she taught her to swim. She kind of mothered her. My daughter and I had many talks, often alone and on occasion with a girlfriend included. I answered any and all of her questions honestly, as I believed she would accept my replies. I never believed in skirting issues with any of my children, and when asked a question, I always tried to honor it with as open an answer as possible. I never believed in "Big Secrets!" or skirting issues. And recalling my own youth, I was not about to make my daughter feel that being a woman was anything less than a beautiful thing.

Life went on, and high school was not pleasant. I enjoyed music, I enjoyed my art classes, I enjoyed English; I enjoyed many things, many classes, and I enjoyed some of my teachers. But my math teacher—I couldn't explain to her that I would know the answer, because my mind would work the problem out in my head so quickly, much faster than I could write it on paper, but I would know the answer. She ridiculed me, she accused me of cheating, she accused me of copying other students' papers, and she kept me after school many times, until I finally begged her, "Please, give me the exam in the principal's office, the first thing when I come into school, so you will know that I'm not cheating, so you will know—" I said, "I can't explain to you how I see it, and know the answer, because I can't figure the problem out." I just couldn't figure the problems out in algebra. She finally passed me with a C. She said, she agreed, I was getting the answers, but because I couldn't work the problems out she could only give me a C. So I didn't do well in high school. I really didn't do well in high school at all, in some of my classes.

The summer of my freshman year I was sitting outside with a girlfriend, and Jack Quinn drove by and saw me, and stopped. He had the Southbury Play House at the time, a summer stock play house, and he said to me, "Would you like to be in a play?" I said sure. So that began a couple of plays of summer stock. It was fun, it was the first time I knew what falsies were; I had no idea Mother was flat-chested, and I was beginning to develop. I didn't realize there were women in this world who were flat-chested, who bought bras that helped them look a little better, a little more feminine. But it was a fun thing to do, and that's when I met Ralph. Ralph's family ended up owning the farm that my father grew up on, and Ralph and I would go horseback riding occasionally on Sundays. Ralph was fun to be with. That went on for awhile, a few years. Until the Sunday night, he was sitting at his piano, and I was sitting on the floor leaning on the piano stool, and he said, "Carrie, I'd like to pin you." He was a senior in college at the time, and I was a senior in high school. And with a heavy heart, a broken heart, I looked away from him, and I said, "Ralph, I can't." He said, "Why not?" And I said, "Because I'm pregnant." And I stood up, put my coat on, and we walked out of my grandfather's house. That was the last time I was ever in my grandfather's house, but not the last time I saw Ralph. I didn't see him again for quite awhile, but after I'd married Charlie, we bought a brick ranch on a dead end road just up from Grandfather's house. Ralph continued to ride his horse past my home for a number of years, during which time we spoke infrequently but kindly. Ralph got to know my sons, who would run out to the road to meet him on his horse, and he always stopped and spoke with the boys, always asking them, "How is your mother doing?" The boys would come running into the kitchen and quietly tell me they had seen Mr. B., "and he asked about you." One day Ralph rode by with a young woman; we waved, and that was the last I ever saw of him. God bless him—he was a perfect gentleman and a love never committed. I pray he has now the good life he deserved.

But I digress. Getting back to the war years: we ate lard sandwiches. Later, margarine was developed. It was a white substance, similar to lard, in a plastic bag with a yellow kind of a bubble in it that you broke, and you kneaded the bag, and then you would cut a corner from this bag, and squeeze it out onto a dish. This was the first margarine. I always had fun squeezing the bag and breaking the bubble when it was my turn to do so. I never fully incorporated the yellow into the white, because I liked the marbled effect it took on. I'd squeeze it from the hole I'd make in the corner onto a dish and it was quite pretty: yellow, orange, and white, in various shadings. But I think the thing I enjoyed most was Mother's reaction. It never ceased to cause her anger that the job had not been done to her satisfaction, which was kind of my way of being nasty to her. There were so few things I could do to get back at her without making it obvious I was being naughty. Or perhaps it was just another way to show my power over her. But until margarine, we ate our lard sandwiches, with a little salt and pepper on them. Once we had a cucumber sandwich. It was Heaven on earth. But aside from that, food was very scarce, and rationed.

The vehicles that were on the highway, or the roads, during the war years, had to have their headlights painted black halfway down, so that the light from them at night shone only on the road and could not be seen from above where there was the possibility that enemy airplanes might be able to see them, or follow them, or track them. Since the factories and foundries etc. were working 24 hours a day, it was necessary for people to drive at night, but it was also necessary to protect them, and this was how this was done. The vehicles were all painted in dark colors. It seemed even the clothes that people wore were drab and dark. It was really a sad time, it was really a very difficult time.

Mother's cooking during those years was really something. It was either too salty or it had too much pepper in it. Mother had no control over her hand when it came to salting or using pepper. The three of us little girls would sit around the kitchen table, and during the good years, as I had mentioned, many times we would pass our food from one to the other to the other, and out the window it would go, to the poor dog. But that was my Pal. She always ate everything. If we didn't eat it, and the weather wasn't good enough to leave the window open, it was put into the refrigerator, and if we had breakfast the next morning—which was a rare thing—it was last night's leftovers. That's what Mother thought was breakfast, with a comment, "Well, you didn't eat it last night, you're going to eat it for breakfast or you don't get anything." Sometimes we did eat it for breakfast, and sometimes we didn't get anything. We never had shoes, we never had new clothes; everything was hand-me-downs, whatever our neighbors, whatever our older sisters, our older siblings, or older cousins, had—and there was always Grams off to a rummage sale. This was all there was. I remember a Christmas during the War years. I'd wanted a doll carriage so badly, and I did get one, but it was made from cloth, a very thin cloth, not a cheese cloth, but a very thin cotton cloth, and it too was of dark color. I had always imagined a wicker one, styled after what I envisioned was a pram. The word sounded so pretty in my ears when I read it in the book by Lewis Carroll called *Alice in Wonderland.* I thought, what a delight to have lived in the Victorian days in England, when things were free and carefree, and everyone was happy. What a delight that would have been, when a child was loved, and wanted.

Anyway, the music that was played was mostly patriotic music. A little jazz, but mostly patriotic music, played on the radio, because of course there wasn't television yet, on 78-rpm records, one record at a time. The 33's came out in the early 50s. Mother, when dressed up, wore chunky shoes and silk stockings, with elastic garters that she would pull up mid-thigh, pull the stockings on, and roll down just above the knees. She didn't wear garters that were suspended from her corset as my grandmother always did (and did till the day she died) but Mother wore these strange elastic things that clung to her legs, but it didn't do her much good at any rate. Skirts were getting shorter, therefore when a woman sat down, the skirts, cut on the bias, always rode up, and the garters were exposed. I suppose men thought that was sexy. I suppose. I thought it was pretty terrible, myself. Pancake makeup was just being developed, although Mother never wore anything but a very powdery stuff, and her lipstick. She never wore anything on her eyes, she never wore any rouge. She didn't have any—she had no style whatsoever. She just had nothing.

There were at that time what were called draft-dodgers. We had a scandalous family in town, of which the whole school spoke disgustedly. They had quickly packed up and left for Canada, not returning until the war was over. The men who had done that sort of thing were not called conscientious objectors at that time, but cowardly draft dodgers. They were really looked down upon and greatly scorned. Although money was everywhere, there was nothing to buy, as all the factories and foundries were converted into war effort manufacturing. Plane parts, tank parts, rifle parts, clothing for our service men and women, that sort of thing. These things were far more important than the home front necessities. Somehow we got by, we would get by. It was our fighting people that were important; we all knew that, even the little children understood and accepted that. They were the ones who were important; they were protecting our country from the ravaging hordes of Nazis or—excuse me if I use the term, but I do use it as it was used then—the Japs.

As I previously mentioned, after the war Dimitri entered my existence, by way of school. He was such a pathetic dear little boy, probably a few years older than myself, but in my need to be needed, I looked upon him as an equal. Teaching him was an experience I shall always recall. I felt the sameness in him that I was experiencing. Two lost lonely little souls in search of a little peace, of happiness, of family, of pleasantness, and of love. So we reached out to one another, almost with blind childish understanding, he having lost his family, and I feeling I had none. Obviously neither of us knew each other's stories, since there was a language barrier, but we were there for each other, as only two little innocent children could be.

The school was kept warm in the winter by a potbellied wood stove in the center of the room. The wood was carried in by the older boys as often as was needed, and the room was kept comparably warm, certainly a little warmer, I do believe, than the house I lived in. And the bathrooms were outside. There were no commodes, as I recall.

School continued on. I was very busy, I was working at home, working at school very hard. I enjoyed grammar school very much, and I had belonged to the Girl Scouts, was very in tune with much of what was going on around me. I was allowed to go into the yards of the little girls in the neighborhood and play, but they were not allowed to come into my yard to play. I didn't understand then why, but the scandalous behavior in my house was known throughout the whole town.

Anyway, it was June of 1950 when I graduated from eighth grade and the Korean War broke out. I was photographed and fingerprinted by the local police for the FBI so I could do my stint as an airplane spotter. The lookout tower was in a field on a very high hill in town. I was afraid of heights, but I could identify the type and direction of any and all aircraft in the area. After all, the Cold War was on. Therefore, nothing got past any of us volunteers—two hours daily, four to six p.m., I worked. We covered the field, recognized the importance of even so minor a thing as watching for airplanes, as identifying an airplane and the direction from whence it came and where it was heading. Mother, of course, didn't approve, but when you're up in the tower alone with only a phone and a pair of binoculars, every plane moving had to be called in and reported on as soon as possible. What the heck kind of mischief could you get into? That summer, on a very warm day, I was wearing a pair of shorts, and a local professional photographer stopped, saw me, and decided to shoot photographs of me which were sent to "Stars and Stripes" in Korea, under the title "Even the Very Young at Home Are Doing Their Stint." I wasn't impressed. It got me legitimately away from the house, with nothing to think about except airplanes for two hours a day. For me it was a break. At home there was always the cooking, the cleaning and the laundry, and homework. I used to think, some day I'll marry well, and I'll have a maid. That too never happened, but so much more was yet to be.

High school was only another form of hell for me. I didn't make many friends, and I didn't date anyone from school. I always thought it was because I was not very pretty. I didn't know the underlying causes of being ostracized until much later. The real reason simply was that everyone in the area was aware of the situation and events created by my parent over my sisters, and my peers' parents simply didn't want that kind of trouble on their doorsteps.

Always having been a small-boned and small type person, I played the ingénue at the summer stock playhouse, and it really was fun. I met real Broadway theater people, and I learned for the first time in my life what padded bras and falsies were, as all the females shared the same dressing room. Living with Mother, who was built like an ironing board, I assumed all adult women, if they had good bodies and shapes as teenagers, simply lost it as mothers and adult females. I was very self-conscious of my own body. After all, wasn't it my own mother who distinctly told me how homely I was? Actually she said I was, and that no one could ever want me. One tends to become withdrawn into oneself after years of that type of emotional assault. Later in life, I realized that not even the man I married ever told me I looked good. When we dressed to go out I would ask if I looked all right, and all he ever said was, "I guess so." I just never seemed to please anyone; therefore Mother must have been right. I finally got to the point in life where I would tease Mother by telling her I was made with spare parts, so why did you bother to have me? I yet had to learn that Mother had had two abortions. God forbid—if any of my children had ever asked me that, I simply would have answered, "You were born because I loved you, and always will." For Mother that wasn't a truism. She never wanted brats hanging off her, and never let us near her to sit on her lap to get a hug, never kissed us, at any age. She lived to be 88 years old, and never knew how to love. What a sad requiem.

During my senior year I met a few people who were a little older than myself, and kind of fell into the crowd, went out with them a few times that fall—in a group, always in a group. That was where I met a nice seminary student, but I really didn't look at him as a boyfriend, I simply looked at him as a seminary student. He had come home to bury his father, and he was to go back, and when he went back he was to graduate, or be ordained, the following spring. We went to a Christmas party, and he was taking me home, but unfortunately he had gotten drunk, extremely drunk. We were in a city I was not at all familiar with, and he pulled into a park, got sick to his stomach. It was a very bitter cold evening, and I sat at my side of the car, leaning against the car door with my coat wrapped around me. He sat slumped over the steering wheel, unconscious. The next thing I knew, I had fallen asleep, and he was on me—slapping me around, it wasn't pleasant, and all I kept thinking was, please dear God, not my face, please dear God, not my face. He weighed 220 pounds and was six foot four. I finally submitted.

Within a couple of months I knew, and Mother was aware of the fact that I was pregnant. I have a way of keeping my worst emotional pains to myself. There was no one to confide in. Even Grams had remarried and was by then living in Vermont, and my sisters had their own lives. Obviously, I did not finish high school at that point. I later went on and got my GED and a few years later went to college, after my marriage and divorce. Prior to that I had already passed my college boards. The baby's father called me, probably February or March, and suggested that we get married, and I said No. All I could think of was, I will not marry anyone who is going to beat me. I will not have anything to do with anyone who would hit me or get drunk—and I never saw him again. I never wished him ill, I never wished him anything; I just wanted him out of my life. But I was grateful, in one sense, because I was pregnant, and for the first time in my whole life that

I can remember, I had a reason to get up in the morning. I had a reason to survive each day, to fight for myself, to struggle through. I had a real reason. I was carrying my baby. The father of my baby didn't matter. The only thing that mattered was my baby, and no one was going to take it away from me.

I was taken by my parents to an abortionist in New York. The doctor, if that's what he was, was not clean at all. The bed that he told me to take my clothes off and lie down on was spotted, stained, soiled; the room was very grubby. It was upstairs, there wasn't an elevator, we had to climb the stairs, and I thought on the way, please, dear God, please, dear God, please dear God, not this, not this, don't let them take my baby, don't let them take my baby, my one reason to live. It was at that point and during those days that I became very close to God. I put my trust and my faith in God and my life in His hands. I began to talk to God as you would a friend. God was really the only friend I had at that time. God was the only one who knew it all, the whole truth.

Through the years, since then, God and I have gotten to know one another pretty darn well. I talk to Him daily. He doesn't of course answer me; he hasn't answered anyone since Moses. But nevertheless when I talk to God a thought will come into my mind, and it will be God's answer to me, or he will direct me to a book, or He will direct me to stop and speak with someone on the street and during the course of that conversation, whoever it is will suddenly say something that may not seem to them out of the ordinary, but it will be the answer to the question I have presented God with. I began to see things. I began to see things ahead of me in time, things other people couldn't see, and I thought, I can't tell anyone about this, they'll think I'm crazy. But it was God showing me things. I recall one day seeing myself walking down the street, carrying a little boy in my arms, a baby boy in my arms, and holding another little boy, about three years old, by the hand, walking down the street. I could even see the clothes they were wearing. The day that did happen was very striking, because it was like deja vu. I had seen it, and here I was experiencing it.

I had married and had given birth to my second son when a cousin was to be married. I had Grandfather with me and my sons. Grandfather and I were walking toward the church when I was overcome with the knowledge, "I've done this before." I abruptly stopped and caught my breath and explained it to my grandfather. He laughed and said, as if he'd expected it, "You have the seeing." He made it seem normal, acceptable. This has happened throughout my lifetime. I do accept it and expect its occurrence at each turn in my path.

But at any rate, God and I began to get very close, and I began to really sincerely, deeply, pray, because my fate was developing, as my baby was developing in my body. I dressed quickly and went out to the anteroom where this doctor, and I say that word advisedly, was speaking with my parents. I was about to tell them, "If you leave me here you will never see me again." I didn't know whether or not I was saying it will kill me, or whether I was simply saying, I will simply disappear out of your lives. But I knew if they left me there, I would never want ever to see either of them again. The doctor was saying to them, "I'm sorry, taking the fetus is one thing, but she's too far gone, and I will not have the blood of a young girl on my hands." Therefore, Mother and Dad took me home.

I ended up at St. Agnes' Home, and it was a lovely place to be for a girl in my position. The prayers were very lovely, the garden was very lovely—it was a beautiful place to be, actually, except for one thing. They wanted my baby, and this was not going to be. This was never going to be. I only spent two weeks there when I called Charlie, and said, "Please come and get me tomorrow, I can't stay here any longer." He asked me, "Where are you?" I told him, and he said, "How can you get out?" I said, "The door is not locked, the gates are not locked. I will be outside at a specific time. Meet me here." And he came and he picked me up. I left my clothes and that world behind me. He said to me, "Where will you go?" I said, "Home." We drove back in silence, and he left me at home. I didn't know what was going to happen; there had already been threats of "Nick, beat it out of her, beat it out of her." My father said, "No, I can't do that. But she's got to give this baby up. She's got to get rid of this baby. She's created a bad scandal for this family." I think in later years, and look back on what he had done to the family, what Mother had done to the family, and I think, an unwed mother bringing such scandal to a family who had already been so scandalously spoken of throughout two or three towns was far less than what had already transpired.

Anyway, I eventually ended up at an aunt's house—my aunt, my godmother, took me in, and then I had my baby. My beautiful baby. When my contractions began with the birth of my first-born, I had the usual showing and a slight backache. I was with my aunt, and I woke her up, not being very much aware of what was occurring. The time was right, but with the first baby, and being a true novice, I wasn't certain what was going on. By 8:00 a.m. that Labor Day morning, I was taken to the hospital, and met by my wonderful doctor. After examining me, he declared, "We'll get this over with by lunch!" And proceeded to unwrap and put his cigar unlit in his mouth. I later learned from experience that one could perceive his concern and my progress by how quickly his cigar was being eaten and shortened. During my labor he said, "Carol, you don't have to suffer the pain without screaming or showing some sort of suffering." I could hear up and down the hall various curses, oaths, and screams from other women, some cursing God, some cursing their husbands, others merely screaming. This was not for me. I quietly explained to Dr. Goldys, "You must understand, with each pain or contraction it brings me nearer to the end, to the moment when my baby will be in my arms. God's miracle. I can stand it. I look forward to each pain. I love the pain."

My baby weighed 8 pounds ten ounces and was 22 inches long, and as Doctor Goldys had predicted, he was born at 11:45 a.m. that Monday morning, before lunch. And I had my miracle, my baby, and he was worth every moment of living through a difficult time. My son was healthy and beautiful and perfect in every way. I loved him before he was born, but with the moment when he was placed in my arms, as weak as I was, I loved him even more. That love has never faltered. He is a fine man, and I never regretted the fight I had with my parents to keep him. He was mine, and a sincerely real reason to go onward. Go on where, I didn't know. I had faith in God that He had seen us through this far, and He wouldn't leave us now. Somehow we'd manage, my baby and I. You see, I was a 19-year-old unwed mother, and it was 1955. This was a scandalous thing for my family. Somehow, not for me. No one knew the circumstances of how I became pregnant; no one asked. My mother told my father to beat me until I aborted, I was taken to the abortionist, and yet I continued to pray, God, let this not be. Please, let this not be. I prayed for God's help and guidance, that I not be separated from my baby. He was the one reason that I first began to fight for my life, he was my one reason to go on living. The fact that I was forced into submitting to someone that I hardly knew was not important. The only important thing was that God had given me another life to care for and love. And therefore I had my reason to go on, not to give up. Although as the course of my life had progressed to this time, I was always a fighter, not one to easily give in or up.

After Jon was born, Mother and Dad wanted me to leave him at the hospital. No way. He was mine and we were never going to be separated. I may have been small, young, weak and naive, but I was very determined. Abortionists at that time were not authorized, probably not even medical; merely people who made money at the price of the unborn and the heartache of those who survived. The sad thing was he had given me an infection, he was so filthy, the abortionist, but God answered my prayers after the examination. I could fight the infection, and when I met Dr. Goldys, he helped me fight the infection. My son was born healthy. You see, God didn't let me down, and he never has.

I tried to explain to Charlie when he was bringing me back from St. Agnes' Home how I had come to this point in my life, and he very quickly and sharply said, "I don't want to know anything about it and I never want to talk about it again." To the day he died he never knew the truth. I believe only God and I knew the truth. I'm not even certain that seminary student realized the truth. He was drunk when it happened. I never felt badly toward him, I only accepted that this was just another phase into which my life's experiences had taken me.

And so the next chapter of my life began.

CHAPTER III

The Married Years

"There are times when even to live is an act of bravery."
Seneca, c. 4 B.C., 65 C.E., Rome.

Charlie's suggestion was that I marry the man responsible for my pregnancy, divorce him after the baby was born, and then he and I would get married. I said "No." The thought of living with someone who would abuse me, any more than I had already been abused—No. I could not do that. I could not explain that to him, and he had said to me on that drive home from St. Agnes' Home, "My mother suggested that this is the way you handle it." I quietly said, "No, this is not the way to handle it. I will have my baby, alone!" And when my baby was born and his birth certificate information came to me, I gave my name and my parents' name, and when it came to stating my baby's father's name, the doctor was standing there, and I looked at the woman taking the information, and when she said "Father's name," I said, "Unknown." Dr. Goldys looked at me, put his hand on my shoulder, and said, "Carol, you can't do that. Do you know what that looks like?" I didn't care what it looked like. I only cared that if the father was unknown on the birth certificate then no one in God's world would be able to legally interfere with my baby's and my life. No one would ever be able to legally take my baby away from me. And there it was stated. As ugly as it may seem, as ugly as it may sound: "Father unknown" was the way I meant it to be.

Anyway, I went home, and when Jon was nine months old, Charlie and I married, in his church. It was his mother's request that we marry in his church, not my church but his church, and I agreed to it. I thought, "He rescued me, this I will do for him." The minister stood and began reciting the funeral doctrine, and realized he had the wrong book in his hand, and with fluttering gown he went running down to his office, with a little "Oh my, oh my, I have a funeral book, I'm reciting the funeral doctrine! This is not the marriage service!" I looked back at my father, and my father had a big grin on his face, and I started to giggle, but I should have known then, I should have known then; this was an omen. This really was an omen. The little minister came back with the proper book in his hand and proceeded on with the marriage ceremony, and Charlie and I were married, on May 18, 1956.

We went off to our honeymoon, and the first night of our honeymoon was about as romantic as anything could be. We had an argument. There was a championship fight on television that night, Charlie wanted to watch it. He did not want to make love, as two newlyweds should have done, he wanted to watch the fight. I went to sleep, without having made love. That was my wedding night. Charlie sat and watched the fight. Our honeymoon took us into Canada and then to our new home, with my son, who had been taken care of by Grams while we were gone. I didn't feel comfortable leaving my baby with my mother and father and had asked Grams to come from Vermont to care for him while I was away.

So life went on, and after a few months of marriage, Charlie suggested—it was his suggestion—that he adopt Jon. I was very grateful for that, so Jon would have the same name as any other children that God would bless me with. I wanted to get pregnant again; I felt I owed it to Charlie to give him a son of his own. I tried to get pregnant. I tried many times to get pregnant. In the course of events, Jon had been adopted by Charlie, and I had lost a baby. It was not meant to be just yet. Jon was two years and eight months old when I finally had my second son. That was a very difficult pregnancy and my second son, my little Scotty, was born without a heartbeat. The doctor was going to put me out after I had delivered my baby, and I said, "No, Dr. Goldys, don't do that, don't do that, let me have him, let me have him." The still quiet little body uttered no sound, and I said, "Isn't there some kind of needle you can give him, isn't there a shot, isn't there something you can give him to make his heart beat?" Suddenly, Dr. Goldys looked, and said, "Adrenalin. We'll give him a shot of adrenalin." They gave him a shot of adrenalin. In those days babies were not placed with mothers in their rooms, they were placed in nurseries. I asked Dr. Goldys, "Please, Dr. Goldys, please let me keep my baby with me." I knew if I kept him with me and was able to keep my hand on him, I would be able to keep him alive. I had to give Charlie his son. I could not lose this baby. I owed it to Charlie to give him a son of his own.

The baby was kept in my room and I would reach out to him, caress his little chest to feel his breathing. I did not realize that I was actually helping him and giving him my energies, my strength, and I was helping him to live. I loved my babies. I really loved my babies. They had to live. They had to make it through life. Scotty's first year was very difficult for the poor little guy. He was very sick. I carried him, I did not simply lay him down and walk away, I carried him. I carried him all over the house. He was sick; I fed him, I loved him, I nourished him. The doctor had said to me so often, "Carol, I can't understand how he's gaining weight and how he's growing and developing so well when he's so sick." But Scotty grew, with my faith Scotty grew, and with God's help and God's guidance, Scotty developed. The doctor had said, with Charlie in the room, "Carol, this little guy doesn't have much of a chance. You have a choice. You can treat him carefully as an invalid and he may grow to be an adolescent and eventually end up in a wheelchair, but probably will not grow beyond adolescence, his heart is too weak. He's just not strong enough. Or you can let him develop as any normal child and take the chance that he will grow beyond adolescence and be strong and healthy." I looked at Dr. Goldys, and I knew in my heart what I would do. This baby was going to be strong and healthy. He was going to be able to play and to run and to frolic and to climb trees. He was going to be normal. I knew in my heart God was with us. This baby was going to be normal. He's close to 40 years old now. I was right. I trusted in God, and once again God did not let me down. God did not let me down. Scotty was a normal little boy—he climbed trees, he ran, he played, he played very good baseball; he was really good at what he did. He learned to swim, he learned to play, anything and everything. My Scotty grew to be one hell of a great young man, and I'm very proud of him and his accomplishments today, just as I am as proud of Jon and his accomplishments today. They have survived and they will continue to survive, and in a way my sons and my daughter would be my legacies, because I have had the faith, and I have never turned my back on that faith, and those prayers, that God would be with us all, which I know He is.

The first Christmas after Scotty was born I bought a toy box for him and Jon, and I said to Charlie, "Please put it together," and Charlie said, "Oh hell, it can wait for a few more days, we have plenty of time before Christmas." I mentioned it to him a couple of more times, "Please put the toy box together," and he put it off and put it off, and Christmas Eve came and the toy box still had not been put together. We had company from the neighborhood that Christmas Eve, and I finally said, "Dear, you've got to put this toy box together," and he and a neighbor started working on that toy box. That toy box was never completely finished, the cover was never put on it, it just sat on it. They worked until two or three o'clock in the morning before my neighbor left and Charlie came to bed. He was too drunk to know how to read the directions, to understand what he was doing; he was just too drunk. Charlie was starting to drink, very heavily, by that time.

A few years later, when Scotty was probably seven or eight years old, he wanted a bicycle, and the bicycle came unassembled, and Charlie had decided Scotty had to put it together. He made Scotty work on that bicycle until ten thirty or eleven o'clock that night, and I went out to the garage and said, "Dear, let Scotty go to bed. He's got school in the morning. Please, can't this wait for another night?" Charlie was drunk, and he said, "No, goddamn it, he's going to learn how to do things for himself, he's going to grow to be a man." And I looked at him, and I said, "Please, let him go to bed. He has to go to school tomorrow morning. Let him go to bed. The bicycle can wait." Charlie just looked at me, and I knew it was a hopeless situation, and I walked back into the house, and I went into bed, and I prayed, "Dear God, please, guide that little guy's hands. Guide him to put the bicycle together to at least satisfy Charlie, so my son can go to sleep." It didn't seem to be much longer when I heard them come in the house. Charlie had been satisfied. Once again, God had answered my prayers. Scotty went to bed and Charlie came to bed.

The first few years of married life were, I would say, kind of pleasant. Our furniture was second-hand; nothing matched, yet we made do. There was the drinking, but it wasn't constant, it wasn't daily—but it was there. The signs were there, but I didn't recognize the signs.

We would get dressed, we would go out; many times we would go to dinner, we would go to family functions, and we would enjoy ourselves. I thought I loved him; I thought I was in love with him. I misunderstood and mistook my gratitude for love. But I was grateful; he had rescued me. I didn't realize that my rescuer had feet of clay.

Another two years and eight months went by, and my Brian was born. Then a couple of years later, my daughter was born, and I thought, this is my legacy. Charlie had always been very stern with me about not babying the boys, not kissing their booboos, not being able to cuddle, love them, but when he wasn't looking, I would scoot with my little boys, and I would love them and hug them and put them on my lap and hold them to me when they were hurt. He had said to me, "You have a daughter and you can spoil her all you want." Well, God blessed me finally with a daughter, and I suppose in a way I did spoil her. She learned how to swim very early. We had a very large pond in the back yard where we skated in the winter and swam in the summer. It was Jon who taught my daughter how to swim. All of my children became very good at swimming and skating. She learned many things very early. I taught her how to make pie crust "from scratch" before she was in school.

Life was becoming more and more difficult, however. Charlie was drinking more and more heavily. His demands on me were more and more critical; his demands on the children were more and more critical. Today I realize, as I look back, this man was totally abusive, not only to me but to my babies also. There are laws now to protect people like me, children like my children, but I didn't know that then.

I did a lot of volunteer work at the grammar school when the children entered school, and I was at the school on many days. I had come home from getting groceries one day, it was kind of a rainy day and I wanted to put the groceries away and run down and pick the children up at the school bus stop. As I rounded the corner of the hallway to the kitchen, with bags of groceries in my arms, Charlie jumped up from the kitchen table and grabbed me by the throat and picked me up off the floor and began to hit the back of my head against the cabinet. "Where the hell have you been, you fucking bitch? Where the hell have you been? Who the hell have you been with?" I guess I blacked out a little, for the next thing I knew I was lying on the floor, with groceries spread about, and Charlie was looking down at me, and he was laughing. He thought it was quite humorous. I had been nowhere, except at school and simply getting groceries, but that's the kind of life I had with Charlie. Our marriage was not a good marriage.

When we had company with other children, he would make my children go out; it did not matter what the weather was, he would order my children, our children, outside to play. The other children could stay in the house, whether it was snowing, icing, raining, my babies had to go outside to play. They were not allowed to stay in the house. The other children were always allowed to stay in the house. Charlie had a warped sense of values, and it always hurt me. I would say to him, "But dear, it's raining out, it's snowing out, it's icing out," whatever it was, "Can't they stay in?" I was silently begging him that if my children had to go out, can't the other children go out too? If the other children can stay in, can't my babies stay in too?

Life went on, and there were always arguments about clothes. I sewed as much as I could; I did as much for him as I possibly could. The baking I did was not from boxes and prepared foods, everything was homemade, this is the way he wanted it, and it was all right with me. He was never quite satisfied, he always had to comment, "My mother could do this better. Why don't you get my mother's recipe?" His mother was as bad a cook as my mother was, in my opinion. His mother had written to him when he was in Korea during the Korean conflict, "You can't marry Carrie when you get home, because she's different than we are. Those people smell different, and they eat differently." She wanted him to marry the girl across the street from where she lived, he wasn't interested, and his proposal to me was really quite simple. We were together one evening, and he said, "I get along with you as well as I get along with anyone else, probably better than anyone else. We may as well get married." And out of gratitude I said, "All right." But it was his mother who chose the wedding day, just as she had chosen the church. My wedding date was on her birthday. I didn't know that until our first wedding anniversary, when he told me it was his mother's birthday. I thought, how unfair, how unutterably unfair. But who was I, who *was* I, to debate it, to argue it. I just went on.

His drinking got worse, and got to be a daily occurrence. His demands got worse, his lovemaking got worse, got more abusive, until one night he demanded of me that I do something that I was not willing to do, and I said to him, "This hurts. I can't do it." He was attempting to sodomize me. He said, "Oh, fuck you," and got off of me.

Shortly thereafter, I was sleeping when he came home—he wasn't coming home until 10 or 10:30 at night—and one night he came in and he demanded that the children be awakened and brought out to eat dinner with him. I said, "But dear, the children have already been fed, they're sleeping, they have school tomorrow. I can't wake them up. I can't bring them out. Just eat your dinner, I'll clean up the kitchen, you go to bed." "No, god damn it," he said. "Get those kids out here." I put my hands on my hips and looked at him and I said, "I will not wake my babies up and get them out here just to satisfy your ego. You can get home at a reasonable time, there is no reason why you cannot get home at a reasonable time. If you want to have dinner with the family you can be here on time." I won that argument, also.

Came the time when his mother, who was widowed, decided she wanted to spend three months with me and three months with another daughter-in-law. I was presented with that proposition, and I held my ground firmly and I said, "No way. I have a mother and father. The day may come when I will be the one taking care of my mother and father. Your mother has a daughter. Let her take care of her. There is nothing the matter with your mother. She does not need care."

At one point when my daughter was around two years old we had left my mother-in-law to baby-sit at our home and we had gone to Massachusetts to visit with friends. We got back and my mother-in-law met us at the door and said, "Charles! Look at my head!" There was a little bit of a blood spot on her head and my daughter was standing behind her saying, "Grammy was in your bureau drawers, Grammy was in your bureau drawers, Mommy. Grammy was in your bureau drawers." Evidently my mother-in-law had been snooping, and I knew when that proposition came toward me from my husband that his mother stay with me for three months, and three months with my brother-in-law, I knew that I would have not privacy, and I looked at my husband and I said, "No. No way will I live with this woman. No way will I be under the same roof with this woman. No way." She never liked me, she never liked my children, she never wanted anything to do with anyone but Scotty. Scotty was the only one she wanted anything to do with. The rest of my children meant nothing to her. I meant nothing to her. In a way, she made my life hell. She pulled my husband between herself and his obligations and his duties toward his wife and his family, and I felt she was the one who was putting him in a position where alcohol was numbing him. It was his choice to drink, but it was his way out. I would not have any part of her living with us. Eventually the day came when I did take care of my mother and father, but I never took care of my mother-in-law. I never would and I never did. That was for her daughter to do, not for me.

Anyway, a year or so later, I was in bed sleeping, my husband's dinner was prepared for him, the children were sleeping, and the next thing I knew, my husband tried anal sex on me again. He had climbed into bed with me. I suddenly sat up and looked at him and I said, "Go fuck your mother," and took my pillow and went out on the sofa. I said, "Don't ever come near me again. Don't ever touch me again." And that was the end of our marriage. It was another couple of years before I actually divorced him, but our marriage was over. There was no more lovemaking, there was no more sex, there was no more anything. There was really no more communication. It was over.

I have learned since—as a Reiki master, teacher, working with many women who have gone through similar situations with the men in their lives—that that happens to be one of the favorite things that woman will say to a man, "Go fuck your mother." It seems to be the only way a woman can get through to a man that the marriage is over. The relationship is over. We are through. Don't ever touch me again. I don't know where those words came from that night, but they did come, and I began sleeping either with my daughter or on the sofa. One night several months later I was watching the Ed Sullivan show, he was in bed, it was a Sunday night, and he came out with an erection, forcing it in my face, and I woke up abruptly, seeing him standing there, and he was ordering me, "Get into that bedroom." I looked at him—and this was long before the Bobbitt situation—I looked at him and I coldly said to him, "Keep that thing away from me, or I'll take the meat cleaver to it and flush it down the commode." He looked at me and he said, "Fuck you, you bitch," and stormed off down the hall, slamming the bedroom door after him. I went back to sleep, and I thought, I am safe. He will never do that again. But I had told him, before he left the room, I said, "From now on, you'd better sleep with one eye open." I did say that to him.

I could see that his cruelty was not only directed at me but at my children as well. He thought only of his own wants, his own needs, his own desires, and the things that his mother wanted. Thinking of his children, he was concerned only about their accomplishments that he could boast about to his drinking cronies. My little Scotty had had pneumonia, but there were days when I would go to the hospital without Charlie—because he was too busy, doing other things, with his drinking cronies. He was too busy getting drunk, and I couldn't wait for him to get home. I had to go to the hospital to be with my little Scotty.

There was the time when my daughter had pneumonia, when she was 14 months old, and he was out hunting with a friend of his. That was more important than going to the hospital to be with our daughter, our only daughter. He had to go hunting; it was more important. I didn't see it that way, I saw my daughter as being the most important thing in my life, with my sons. He had said to me, "Wait until I get home, we'll be back around noon, and then we'll go to the hospital." It was on a Saturday, "We'll go to the hospital together." I said to him, "All right, I'll wait until noon." And I waited until noon, at which time he arrived home and he said to me, "My buddy's dog didn't come back; we've got to go back in the woods to find her." This was many towns away. I looked at him and I said, "My daughter is in the hospital, my baby is sick in the hospital. I've got to go to her." And he said, "It can wait. We've got to go get the dog." He was putting a dog, his friend's dog, before my daughter? Where were his priorities? What was this man thinking? What was going on in his mind? Yes, he once again, as usual, was drunk, but what was going on in his mind? I went to the hospital without him. He and his friend and the dog were waiting for me when I got back from the hospital, and he was furious with me. He was raving and ranting and screaming at me, "You stupid bitch! What did you go to the hospital for without me? You knew I was coming back!" Hospitals have visiting hours. They have times when you're allowed in and times when you're not allowed in. I had to get to my daughter. I had to get to my baby. Nothing was going to stand in my way. I said nothing to him that night. I said nothing to him. I fed my sons and just looked at him, and said, "When you get around to eating, your dinner is on the stove." And my sons and I went into the living room and left him to sit and finish drinking his night away as he cursed me as I walked away from him. As far as I was concerned, he too could go to hell.

Came the Sunday of the accident with the lawn mower and my daughter. I believe she was in second grade. School had just begun the week before and he was out mowing the lawn, drunk as usual. He ran over her foot with the lawnmower. He did not know that she too was born with a heart problem. (I had asked the doctor to please not let him know. I begged Dr. Goldys, please not let him know that she had a heart problem. After going through with my mother-in-law what I had gone through, and with him, trying to make an invalid of my son who was developing strong, healthy and wholesome, I was not going to let them do that to my daughter.) He came in with my daughter, holding her in his arms, and I looked at her, and I wrapped up her foot, and called the doctor's service, and let him know we were on our way; there was a lawnmower accident, my daughter's foot was very badly injured. By this time, having raised three sons, believe me, this particular doctor was very familiar with us, and our broken bones. He met us at the hospital and he checked my daughter over. She was in shock, he checked her over and he said, "She has a very serious heart murmur." It was the first time my husband had ever known about it, and he wanted to kill the doctor. He jumped up and grabbed the doctor by the throat and the doctor called security. Security came and the doctor said to me, "Get him out of here." He said, "I'll do the best I can with your daughter." And I looked at my daughter lying there unconscious, and I looked at my husband being held back by two security guards at the hospital—I didn't know—I was torn between two loyalties: to get him the hell out of there or to stay with my daughter. The doctor put his arm around me and said, "Carol, get him home, get him out of here, get him home. I'll do the best I can with her, and I'll take care of her the best way I can." I didn't want to leave her. My heart wanted to stay with her. I felt the closer I was to her, the more I could give her of myself, and bring her through this. The doctor said to me, "Carol, go home. I will call you as soon as we're out of surgery. Just get him out of here." I had no choice. I had to get him home, I had to get him out of the hospital and away from the doctor. The doctor had a job to do, and that job was very important; repair my daughter's foot.

I took Charlie home. He went to bed, flopped across the bed, and I sat waiting by the phone, dozing, and looking at the clock, dozing and looking at the clock, waiting for the phone to ring, which it finally did, and it was the doctor. He told me of the damage that had been done to my daughter's foot, but he said she was in recovery, she had made it through surgery. My prayers had been answered. God knows how I prayed. God knows how deeply I believed and I prayed. I couldn't be with her, but I knew God was with her. He wouldn't take her away from me after having given her to me.

The next morning I woke up very early. I had done much sewing through the years, and I had two remnants of cloth that I didn't know what I was going to do with. They were very pretty little remnants. One was pink and one was blue and they were floral, and I thought, all this time I've saved these two remnants and didn't know what I was going to do with them. My daughter needs a nightgown. She's got to have a new nightgown when she wakes up this morning. I got up very early and I made her a nightgown. It was so hot that September, it was so very hot, but I made her a new nightgown, with little breezy sleeves, and little lace around the neck, and as the boys were eating breakfast I was hand-sewing the hem, and I left the boys at my neighbors to take to the bus stop, and I went off to the hospital to be there when she woke up. I walked into her room, and she said, "Mom, is that you?" And I said, "Yes, baby girl, it's me." In those days I called her "Pussy Cat." I said, "Mom's got a gift for you, Pussy Cat." She had a hospital robe on, and I got her water and her wash cloth and cleaned her little face and cleaned her little hands and powdered her and got her changed, and put her nightgown on, and she had such a smile on her face. "My mom made a new nightgown for me." New things were really the only things that pleased—there were seldom any new things unless I made them. Charlie would not spend the money on new clothes for the children.

The doctor came in to check her over early that morning; I was standing there and he admired her nightgown and he said, "Wendy, where did you get it?" She said, very proudly, with a smile on her face, "My mom made it, this morning." He looked at me and put his arm around my shoulder and he said, "That's the way good mothers do things for their little babies. That's the way good mothers do things." He gave me a little squeeze. And I stayed with her until it was time to go home to get the boys, meet them at the bus stop.

At the end of her recovery, she had gone back to school, she was on crutches, and by the last time we were to meet the doctor I had made arrangements for her to take ballet lessons. I was not going to have my daughter disabled. She was not going to be disabled. I said to her on the way to the doctor's, that last appointment, after she had healed, I said, "Baby girl, you and Mom are going to have ballet lessons." She was so frightened, she was so worried that the doctor would be angry or say "no;" she had a double-breasted little coat on, but she was so frightened and so worried that she had twisted all of her buttons off of her coat by the time we had gotten to the doctor's office. We looked at the doctor and he said, "Well, she's come along very well. Her big toe is wired and it looks like the wires are staying right in place where they belong." I said, "Doctor, I've signed her up for ballet." He looked at me rather incredulously, and I said, "Yes. She is going to take ballet." I said, "I believe the day will come when she will actually be able to stand on point." And he looked at me and he said, "With your determination, I believe it too."

When she had her ballet recital, the night before, she was in costume, and I stood her in front of the garage on the tarp, and I took pictures of her. I mailed those pictures to the doctor and he put them up in his office. There she was, in her ballet outfit, her leotard, and there she stood, with her little hair piled up on her head, looking as proud as could be. She had come a long way. Her foot was strengthening, and she had come so far. She was not going to be crippled, she was going to be a whole person, and that's what I wanted, and that's what my determination and God's will wanted.

And life went on. There was the Kennedy assassination and the Martin Luther King assassination, and the country was in chaos. We were on the brink of a civil war again, but life went on. One day Charlie came home and dinner was ready, he was drunk, and I went down the hall to let him know that dinner was on the table, and there he stood, across the bed from me, with a .38 pointed right at me. I looked at him and said, very quietly, very calmly, "Go ahead and shoot. You can't frighten me any more than you already have. I'm not afraid to die." He threw the gun down on the bed. "Fuck you," he said. "Get the hell out of here." I quietly said, "Dinner is on the table," and turned around and walked away. I didn't panic, I didn't do anything, I simply turned around and walked away, called the children to dinner, and we sat down and ate. I had said to Charlie, "You're drunk, and if you come home tomorrow night, the very next day I see an attorney. And our marriage will then be over; I will divorce you." The very next night he came home drunk. The day after, I saw an attorney, and I divorced him.

In the interim, during the Vietnam War, I got involved in civil duty work as I had always done, and I had met a gentleman who was a Marine Corps recruiter at the time. I was not against the war or for the war, was only in support of our men in Vietnam. There was so much against the war in Vietnam in our country at that time, but our men needed the support of everyone they could get. And I got involved. One day I was brought to this recruitment office and introduced to him. The door opened and I stood there and I looked across the room. As he stood up from behind his desk, I looked at him, and I thought for the first time in my life, There is a man. There is a man who stands head and shoulders above all men. There is truly a presence. For the first time in my life, I knew what it was to be in love. This was not the love I had felt originally for Charlie that was merely gratitude, this was being in love. And the voice in my head said, "Those whom I have put together, let no man put asunder." And I knew, I knew. And as time went on, he had gone back to Vietnam for the third time, and the letters began to come back and forth between him and me, and the letters got more and more impassioned. I realized that perhaps he too, though he was also married at the time, he too just might be falling in love with me. I was grateful, and I was in love. That love has carried for over 30 years. He is today back in my life. Not in the same way, but he is back in my life. I will always at least be his friend. This is one of the greatest men I have ever known, kindly, compassionately, gently, I loved him. I do love him, and I probably always will love him. Now that I am widowed, if there is going to be a tomorrow for him and me, it is in God's hands. It is His will.

At any rate, I did divorce Charlie, and life went on. This gentleman came back from Vietnam, and he would spend weekends with me, and as time went on he was stationed at the Pentagon and going back to school getting a law degree, and he finally would spend days, evenings, after work, with me and my children at my house. He was kind, he was gentle, he was compassionate, and he was very loving. Nothing I had ever known in my life could compare with the days and evenings I spent with this man. And he was good to my children. I have nothing but the highest regard and the highest respect for this gentleman.

And so another phase of my life was over, and another chapter had begun. I eventually, while I was divorced, moved to Virginia to heal, more than anything else, simply to heal, and spent a year in Virginia, and then I received a call from Charlie. "I'm sick," he said. "Please, can you come back and help me." I had no recourse but to go back to Charlie and help him. After all, he was the father of my children. I still had gratitude toward him; I still had a strange kind of love for him. I went back to him, and another chapter of my life began. And this chapter was over. This gentleman was not in my life any longer. I was back with Charlie.

CHAPTER IV

Second Marriage to the Same Man!

"Those whose minds are filled with kindness will never enter a world dark with woes. No cruel wrongs will ever overtake anyone who protects all living beings and is kind to them."

Tu[?] c. 500, India

The next 23 years there were so many emergency rooms and trips to doctors, there just wasn't enough time for my own life. At one point during the first three years, I drove Charlie, nearly unconscious, to the E.R. and was told kindly by the doctor in attendance, "Mrs. T., why don't you just take him home and let him die in peace!" That was not to be! That was not going to be! And it wasn't.

Although I was working a regular job, I maintained constant watch over Charlie through all those years. I watched him give up alcohol, I watched him through several surgeries, I watched him try to make the house into a home for us and I watched him suffering unmercifully until the end.

So often, when I'd arrive home from work, we'd begin a warm conversation when suddenly he would begin to rave at me. "You fucking bitch, what took you so long to get here? Do you want me to bring a cot down to 'that place' so you can stay there and live there?" Those were times when his arterial sclerosis would click in and his brain would shift into negative. Occasionally, out of pure frustration, I'd shout back at him. "Shut up—please, just shut up!" Other times I'd try to explain why I was a few minutes late. But more often I'd simply turn and leave the room with my collie following, and go into the bathroom, turn on the faucets (water is purifying, and noisy) and sit on the floor praying aloud until it would penetrate my mind that I didn't hear him any more. I'd say, "Thank you, God, he's quiet now." And I'd get up and make a pot of coffee, bringing him a cup and he'd look at me and say, "Where the hell have you been?" And I'd answer, "Just making the coffee, dear. Just getting you your coffee." It would be over until the next time.

He did have that funny peculiar quirk about my cooking. It didn't matter what I was preparing, he felt I should stay in the kitchen, near the stove, while the food cooked. Even if it was beef stew which you can leave simmering and just go to stir it, I had to stay in the kitchen until it was done. I never did figure out that peculiarity of his. I guess it's not important now, but it is something about which I will always wonder. But, I'm pretty eccentric myself: I collect stones.

I came back from Virginia. Charlie was very sick, he was drinking, incredibly enough, a half a gallon of vodka a day. It probably would have killed most people. It only made him sick. There were many trips to emergency rooms, many trips to doctors, and there was always the incessant glass of ice cubes filled with vodka. He drank for another three years, and was very sick. The man was very sick; he needed help. I never nagged him, I never berated him. He was very difficult to get along with. But he needed help, and he knew he could count on me. One day I walked in from work, and he pushed the bottle of vodka away from him, and he said, "Funny Face, I don't need this any more." I looked at him and said, "That's nice." And he said, "No, take it, put it away." I kind of shrugged my shoulders, walked past him, went in to change my clothes, and came back out in the kitchen, made a pot of coffee as usual, and he said, "I'll have a cup." I gave him a cup of coffee. And he said to me once again, "You can put that away." I left that bottle on the table, the rest of that day, all that night, the following morning and all the next day. I came home from work; the bottle had not been touched. It sat where he had pushed it on the kitchen table. At that point, I picked it up and put it in the closet. He never had another drink after that. But this man was very sick. He had been in and out of hospitals; he had been diagnosed with diabetes; he had been diagnosed with many very severe things. And he was suffering from severe neuropathy. He was in pain.

After my divorce, or because of my divorce from him, my family kind of shrugged me off. They thought I was wrong, they didn't know the suffering, the pain, the real hell I had been through and the children had been through living with Charlie and his alcoholism the last years. They had no idea what was going on. I didn't talk of it, I didn't speak of it, I didn't share it with anyone. I kept it to myself. The children kept it to themselves. We just knew there was no one we could turn to, and we stayed in a group.

Going back to Charlie, my family wasn't very happy about that, they didn't want to see me, they didn't want to have anything to do with me. When Charlie got sober, he was a recovering alcoholic. He was put on Percosets for his neuropathy, and he was at that point afraid of addiction. Seems kind of silly, when you think of it, when you've been addicted to alcohol for so many years. But he would very carefully take the Percosets for the pain the neurothropy gave him, and he would sit and he would rub his legs and rub his legs and rub his legs. He was not able to work, his walking got increasingly more and more difficult, and my prayers got stronger and stronger, my faith got stronger and stronger. I believe it all went back to my father's mother, who spent more time on her knees than she ever did on her feet or her back. My grandmother knew how to pray. And I believe that's where I first really learned prayer can do miracles. It was God's will and prayer that made this man stop drinking. There were arguments because he had arteriosclerosis; he was very argumentative, he was very difficult to get along with. But I would not leave him, I would take care or him.

A few years later, my mother and father's 50th wedding anniversary was upon us, and that Sunday morning they were having a big celebration. I went to my mother and father crying; my heart was breaking, I wanted my parents back. I had a man in my life, I was living with him; I wasn't married to him, I wasn't sleeping with him but I wanted my parents back. I wanted my family back. Charlie agreed to this, but at that point my parents were not ready to accept me, and I went home to Charlie's house broken-hearted.

Things went on. Charlie was in and out of hospital, back and forth to doctors, I went to work every day. The two youngest children graduated from school. My third son had gone into the Navy, was in the Gulf War. Charlie, who had been in Korea, was very proud of that. My daughter went on with her life. She graduated from high school, and her life went on. Her story is her own. I won't go into that either. This is my life as I perceive it. This is my story as I lived it, as I remember it, and, dear reader, if you have gotten this far with me, bear with me a little longer.

At any rate, the day came when it was time for me, on Mother's Day, to bring the family together, and I made the phone calls—rather hesitantly, rather nervously, I made the phone calls. Everyone agreed, Mother's Day was ladies' day, we would all meet at a particular restaurant. Everyone sat with bated breath wondering what would happen when my sister and I finally saw each other for the first time in many years. I had my back to the door, sitting at the table, and Mother was across the table from me, and she said, "Here comes your sister." I stood up, and turned, and held out my arms, as she was holding out her arms to me. We hugged one another, and I thank God for that moment. I had my sister, my oldest sister back, and we have been closer than ever, ever since. I thank God for that, and for the faith I had that that day would come.

After living with Charlie for years, Charlie wanted to marry me once again, and I saw no point in that. I was not going to leave him. I would not to walk away from a sick man. I would stay, I explained that to him, and he said, "No, Funny Face, we have got to get married." I casually said to him, "Oh, sure." I came home from work one day and he said to me, "We're getting married next Thursday." I said, "That's nice." He said, "No, seriously." I headed toward my room to change my clothes, and I came back to the kitchen to put the coffee on, and he said to me, "We're getting married in your church." I turned and looked at him and I said, "How can that be? All of my records aren't in this town." He said, "Don't worry about it. I've made all the phone calls, I've made all the arrangements, all the records are here. We're getting married at 7 o'clock next Thursday night." I sat down and looked at him and I said, "You're really serious, aren't you? You know that's not necessary. You know I won't leave you." He said to me, "I feel it's necessary." I thought, Well, if it makes him peaceful, that's the very least I can do. Bring peace to him. Give him the peace that he needs. Physically he did not have peace, he was living in his own hell, but emotionally, the least I could do was bring him peace. And I said, "Okay, I guess the least I can do is buy a new suit." We went shopping for that suit, and I wore it that Thursday night, with three of my children in attendance. You know, the strangest thing: I never saw that suit again. After I got home that night I hung it in the closet, and I never saw that suit again. I don't know where it went. When the closet was cleaned, the house was sold, clothes were given to Good Will, clothes were given to the Salvation Army—I never saw that suit. I don't know where it went, and I never wore it again after that night.

I remember that night very clearly because it brought me back to the first time he and I had gotten married, and I thought, "This poor man is so sick, and so different from the first time we married." I did have a love for him. I can't explain the kind of love I had for him. It wasn't the kind of a love a woman has for a man where she wants a man, she needs a man—it wasn't that kind of a love, and it wasn't the kind of love a brother would have for a sister, or vice versa. It was a strange kind of love. I felt a great deal of compassion for him and I felt very close to him, and it was very easy for me to take care of him. And as time went on, Mother and Dad and I got very close to one another, and Mother and Dad began to lean very heavily on me. Mother's mind was going very quickly, and Dad was getting sicker all the time. His heart was failing. I was able to keep the books and the records and the checkbooks for both Mother and Dad and for Charlie and our home. Charlie did his best for me, Mother and Dad did their best for me.

There were little things. I would go to Dad's house every night after work and say, "Dad, what do you want for dinner tonight?" Or I would call him from work. "Dad, what do you want for dinner tonight? Where's Mother?" "Mother's sleeping. Mother's got a headache and she's sleeping." I would go to their house, having picked up whatever it was Dad wanted from the grocery store and the drug store; I would take Mother and Dad to doctors and take my husband to doctors, and see my husband and Mother and Dad in and out of hospitals. It was hard work, it was difficult, but I managed to do it. With the help of God I managed to do it. But at one point, I picked up the phone one morning at work, and I reached for a phone book, and I looked for this gentleman from my past whom I had known so many years ago, with whom I had not been in contact for so many years. I was reaching out to him. I needed him. I needed his help. I needed the confidence he would give me, that he had given me. I needed it once more. I was a little frightened, and I needed the reassurance that being with him would give me. I couldn't find him. It was not time. God was letting me know, it was not time. I gave up. I knew I had to carry this one on my own. I had three people to take care of, I had two households to take care of, I had cooking to do for three people. It was not easy.

Many nights, many nights I was lucky if I got two or three hours sleep. I became very much accustomed to not getting any rest. It was a very difficult time. Charlie, because of the arteriosclerosis, because of the pain he was constantly in and because of the Percocets, was rapidly becoming very argumentative.

There would be those odd moments when he would be very gentle and very kind. During those last years I was working in a place where the CEO was very cruel, and today I can forgive him for the hell he put me through. He was constantly after me, and I was constantly and always saying, "Just forget it, just forget it." He one day tossed his wallet to me and said to me, "You can have everything that's in it. Come up to my office. I can lock the door, no one will bother us. I'm the CEO." I pushed his wallet back and said, "I know it has been said that every man has his price, but you will never know what my price is, and you will never have enough money for it." I continued working, and every day he made my life more and more hell, and five minutes before he was due in the office he would ooze around the corner and creep up to my office with his requests, and I would refuse him, until one day, one day, he came to my office, stood in the doorway, and said to me, "I want to eat you." And suddenly, I looked at him, and his head wasn't a human head any longer, his head had suddenly—it was a serpent's head. I grabbed my purse, ran out of the building, got to the sidewalk by my car, and vomited. And I went home. On the way home I vomited again. When I got home I had nothing in my stomach; I ended up with the dry heaves. I went to the living room and lay on the sofa. In one of those tender moments that Charlie had, he came over to me and he said to me as I lay on the sofa, curled in the fetal position, he said, "It's ___, isn't it?" I nodded my head Yes. He said, "Do you want to talk about it?" And I shook my head No. He said, "If I could, if I had the strength, I'd go down and kill the bastard." I just shook my head No, and I went to sleep. I went to work the next morning, and some of the beautiful people I worked with knew what had happened, and from that time until the end of the CEO's life, he was never in my office without someone waiting and coming into my office before he got there. They always knew when he would come oozing down those stairs, and creeping into my office, and a few minutes before he was due to do that, there would be someone in my office, protecting me. You see, God does answer prayers and send his angels. I had many friends in that building, and they all protected me from him. I never experienced anything like that again. I never did anything to encourage this sort of thing. But it did happen. And poor Charlie was frustrated because there was nothing he could do. In his early days he probably would have gone out and killed him. But at this time in his life there was nothing he could do. But the comfort he gave me, for that brief moment, brought me enough peace so I went to sleep, and I slept very soundly for a couple of hours, peacefully and soundly, with his hand on me. He gently put something over me to cover me, and said, "Poor Funny Face."

A few years later, toward the end of Charlie's life, he looked at me one day when I had come back from Mother and Dad's house and I said to him, "Just let me sleep for about 20 minutes. I'm very tired, just let me sleep. I'll be all right in about 20 minutes and then I'll get dinner going." And he looked at me and he said, "Poor Funny Face. I wish it were over for the three of us so you could be at peace at last, and get on with your life." I raised my hand and said, "Just let me sleep. I'll be all right, dear, I'll be all right." And I slept for about 20 minutes, then woke up, got up, got dinner, and life went on.

Mother got more and more depraved, Dad got sicker and sicker, Charlie got sicker and sicker, and one day I got the call from Dad, "I need help, Carrie. I can't get your mother back on her bed." I ran to the house that morning. Mother had had—I don't know if it was a stroke, I don't know what it was, but Mother was out of it. She was virtually comatose. I called 911, got Mother into the hospital, and a couple of days later I began to have my own symptoms, which I ignored. There was no time for me to think of myself. The doctors had said to me, "There's nothing we can do. She either has to go home or she has to go to Hospice. There's nothing more we can do here in the hospital for her. She's dying." I said to the doctor, "Well, bring her home. She always wanted to die at home. We'll bring her home." We brought her home, and when the registered nurse from Hospice came into the house she looked at me and said, "I think you'd better see a doctor. You don't look good." That's when I knew that I myself was having a heart attack. That's when I knew I myself was facing a serious condition.

Four days later, I had angioplasty and a stent put in. A few minutes after I got home the phone rang, my daughter answered the phone, and it was the registered nurse from Mother and Dad's house. Mother had gone ten minutes before that. And a few months later Charlie was in the hospital, he had a heart attack and bypass surgery—he was home only a couple of weeks when he became critical. He had had the shunt put in and was on dialysis. He woke me up one morning at three o'clock, and I said, "I can get you to the emergency room, I can get an ambulance." He said to me, "Just let me go. I'm ready. Just let me go, I can't take any more. But don't tell Scotty." Scotty was living at home at the time. Scotty came downstairs and I said nothing to him, I showered and dressed as if I were going to work, as though there were nothing wrong, and Scotty went off to work, and Charlie and I had a long conversation. Charlie was—it was as though he were in both worlds at the same time, seeing things very clearly for the first time. He said to me, "Funny Face, you've been very faithful, you've been very good to me. I couldn't have asked for anyone better." But he said, "I know where your heart is. Go find him. Get yourself some happiness.

Get out of this house. It's not safe for you any more." I held his hand, and watched him take his last breath and then I called 911.

We were asked to write—one of the children or myself—to write the eulogy for Charlie. I spoke with the children, they refused, they said, "No, Mom, I can't do it." I went to bed the night before his funeral with a heavy heart, and I thought, What can I do now? There has to be a eulogy. I woke up some time during the night, went out to the kitchen, got a pad and a pen, and I wrote Charlie's eulogy. I'll quote it:

> *"Charlie was a man who built his world with the sweat of his brow, the muscle of his arm and the love in his heart. He raised his four children with sternness and integrity and love. He gave us all his honesty and devotion. His love for his family and his friends will carry us all beyond the grave. He is with God, but he is still with us. He loved his granddaughters because he knew they were the hope of tomorrow. They were an extension of his sons and therefore an extension of himself, and through his pain and suffering he welcomed each of the three new lives as they were born. He was a good man, and he died with the belief that his wife's faith in God would give her and her children the strength and courage to see them through their loss. He was a man much loved and will be deeply missed by his wife, family, and friends. Funny Face."*

That was Charlie's eulogy. I went back to sleep, and went to the funeral. Charlie had a military funeral and was put to rest.

A few months later it was Dad's time. Dad had said to me, "Carrie, let me go." I said, "Dad, I don't want to let you go. I've lost two already, I don't want to let you go. I've always loved you, even though sometimes we've been a world apart, I've never stopped loving you." He looked at me, and he said, "Carrie, I know that. I don't know where it comes from, but I've always known that." I got up quietly from the table, gave him a kiss on his head, and I said, "I'll see you tomorrow, Dad." It was only a few days later, Dad was gone. That was when Dad and I actually said goodbye. And Dad was gone, and it was over.

My life began again, alone, facing the future alone, carrying on, and here I write this book, knowing that God is with me, I am not alone. Knowing that God has carried me to this point, He will see me beyond. I have been a caregiver, I have been one who's able to forgive. I learned how to forgive. I learned how to forgive even V., and with the forgiving of even V. came a peace that washed over me like a warm rain, and I felt a contentment, and I was able to pray for him, knowing that he would rest in peace and that it was now between his soul and God, because I have always believed our soul is a golden thread, and it is that golden thread that we must never sever, we must walk in the light. Some people choose to walk in the dark, some people choose to covet money, some people choose to covet possessions. I choose to covet people. I choose to love people. I choose to walk in the light with my hand extended, to help my brother man. That is my choice; that is that path I have chosen. It may be the path seldom trod, but it is my path. And if God so chooses and I walk the path the rest of my days alone, for I know not how many pages are on my calendar, I shall do it knowing that God is with me, and this beautiful man whom I met so many years ago, if he is never going to be in my life, so be it. God is with me. For me that will be enough.

CHAPTER V

How My Faith Came About and
Developed into My Reality

*"Do not go forth where the path may lead, go instead where
there is no path and leave a trail."*
                              Ralph Waldo Emerson, 1803-1882

The infant Jesus of Prague, a statue, or icon if you prefer, dates back I
believe to 1631, when the toddler-aged Jesus appeared to a monk named,
appropriately, Joseph, during the battle between the Moors and the Christians.

Many miracles have been attributed to the prayers to this statue
throughout the world: Asia, Vietnam, India, South America, and of course
Europe and the United States.

It was before a replica of this statue that I would always find my
grandmother praying. There were, of course, other statues in her bedroom,
to which I'm sure she also prayed, but this one in particular was of great
importance to her, and therefore to me. She had brought hers with her from
Italy, and had hand sewn the new clothes for it every year in preparation
for his feast day. Red and white satin trimmed in lace. The sights and
accompanying feelings I had as a child remained in my psyche my entire
life. This was the beginning and the strength of my faith.

I was also fortunate, or blessed, to be born into a deeply religious family
via my dad's family. As a toddler, on the Sundays when Dad would bring
the family to his parents' farm for dinner, I recall entering the old stone
farmhouse where my godmother, Dad's youngest sister, would always greet
me with big hugs and kisses and then, setting me down, let me scamper

through the kitchen to Grandmother and Grandfather's bedroom at the back of the house. I would always hesitate at the door to see my grandmother praying before the large statue of the Infant of Prague. It was a happy place for me, in that house, but the peace and true comforting was always to be found with my grandmother, in her room. That peace would seem to wash over and through me, reinforcing the love God gave me. After a moment or two I would troop into the room and reach out to rest my left hand on her right shoulder. The indomitable feeling I'd get at that moment and while I would remain with her there would erase any negativity I carried within myself. I didn't know God, I didn't know praying, I didn't know the Infant of Prague; all I knew was it was like a magic place from which I didn't want to leave. Almost enchanted!

Grandmother spoke only a very few words in English and certainly her Bible was printed in her language, Italian, yet she had a way of conveying feelings to me, feelings which made me aware of what she wanted of me. She had wanted me to be named Catherine, after St. Catherine of the Miraculous Medal (Dad's family ignored the fact that Mother had rebelled and had named me Carol), therefore Grandmother would look up at me smilingly, "Caterina, come!" Grandmother passed when I was only nine years old, yet her guidance has never left me. Perhaps she was responsible for my strengths and whatever courage I may have and I recognize today that it was she who was responsible for developing my faith.

I can still recall that morning when my uncle came to the house to tell Mother and Dad, "Mom died during the night." I ran to my bed crying with Mother fast on my heels. "What are you crying about? You don't know what dying means." I didn't answer. I didn't know what dying meant? I thought. I didn't know about my sister being put in a cage and taken out of my life? I didn't see my little girlfriend Sylvia struck down by a car, lying in a little heap of broken bones and blood? I didn't know about the crematoriums of which I'd read in the newspapers? I didn't know about the dogs that would go hunting, never to return . . . Oh yes, I knew what dying meant. It meant never again seeing or touching or laughing with someone at something ever again. It meant they were gone out of my life forever. And yet there were always the memories left behind with love in them. And, as you can see, the memory of my dear little grandmother is yet deeply entrenched within my heart and soul.

I was happily blessed at having had Grandfather until after my fourth baby was born. He was in his 80s when he passed, but I feel he will always be with me. After I married we lived in a house whose property adjoined his fields and he would so very often walk with his staff to my home and have lunch with my children and me. Sometimes he would eat soup and a sandwich and sometimes he would eat Italian cheese and pepperoni with the bread, and, of course, always his bottle of wine was on the table. My children adored him—he returned their love unconditionally. After the children ate, they would leave the table with a kiss on his round little face and go off to play and Grandfather and I would spend time sharing his past, his early life, his years and his wisdom. He was kind, loving, sweet, and caring.

One day when my daughter was only a couple of weeks old, Grandfather and the boys were at lunch and my baby awoke; it was time to feed her. I brought her out into the kitchen, sat down and began nursing her. Suddenly Grandfather said, looking at me from across the table, "Caterina, you look like a Madonna." I looked up at him and smiled kind of shyly as he continued. "None of my daughters or any of my other granddaughters feeds the bambinos like you—like my Maria!" His eyes got all watery and he sat quietly, simply watching me. It was one of those sharing moments with deep sentimentality. He was remembering. It was a time to be quiet and let his thoughts travel backward in time to better days.

I, too, was recalling an intimate afternoon shared with him. My firstborn was about a year old when I had received a frantic phone call from an aunt who lived at the beginning of our dirt, dead-end road. Her Holstein cow was calving and in great distress. She couldn't find the vet or Grandfather or anyone and she was panicking. I put Jon in his stroller and walked down to her house. The cow was lying on her side in much distress, moaning rather loudly. This was a new experience for me: what to do? I said to my aunt, "Go sit with her head in your lap and try to keep her calm." It was obvious, even through the blood that was beginning to flow, that this was a breech birth. As I was praying to God and St. Francis for guidance, I was also debating mentally on how to turn this calf around. As I laid my hand onto the cow's stomach I felt for the contractions. Thank God, Grandfather appeared. He said to me, after surveying the situation, "Caterina, you have small hands. Reach in and I'll tell you what to do!" And together we birthed a delightful Black Angus calf. Mother and baby did well. Grandfather taught me much and I was a willing student.

Spirituality I got from my grandmother. But it was compassion I learned from my grandfather.

AFTERTHOUGHTS

Linkages and Relationships
"Lessons to be Learned"
"As you give so shall you receive"

Like a pebble dropped into a puddle, the ripples go outward to the puddle's little shore, one after another, until the end. This is as a link and a relationship. Be it parent and child, friend to friend, business associate to business associate, the ripple effect occurs. Therefore, the effect touches not only the one on one, but carries over to touch those other ones with whom they are confronted.

Just as your pet takes on your personality, your words and your touch are also given to others to create, hopefully, a positive reaction within them and outward and onward to others.

The love of God is a relationship which when fully developed creates a definite link to the universal knowing. The love of children accepts their faults as well as accepting with pride their accomplishments. In loving our children we learn of them as distinct personalities until the day arrives when we view them as equals, people in their own right. People who have the right to lead their own lives as they wish, hopefully to make this a better world. Not people patterned after ourselves, but individuals who are complete within themselves.

Friendships are much the same. Some may last a lifetime during which you may lose touch, but upon seeing one another again it seems you pick up where you left off. Yet some friends you shuck off quickly, recognizing very little in them that equals what is in you.

Business associates on the other hand are more like linkages. People use you too often for their own advantage, to get ahead, to advance themselves or their bank accounts.

The bottom line is life is all a game of chance. Are you willing to take the chance or will you be one of those who "cop out" as in an "overdose" of alcohol or some other way. I have taken many chances and have known some wonderful people and also have had many kicks in the head, yet I continue on, taking one more chance after another. I've found the "pay off" to be always better each time than the last one.

On the subject of parent-children relationships, I should like to expound. The time arrived, which I dreaded, yet looked forward to, when it was time to explain to my son about his adoption. I wanted to be the one to talk to him about it because I felt no one else could tell him with the love I had for him, explain it to him gently and lovingly. I didn't want that information to come from anyone else or possibly to be overheard in other's conversations. That sort of thing could be emotionally devastating to a child.

At about the age of eleven, he and I were in the house alone, the other children were out playing in the yard, and I asked him to come and sit beside me on the sofa. I hesitantly said to him, "Honey, I've got something very important to talk about to you." He sat and looked at me wonderingly. I said, "Honey, your dad is not your real father like he is to the other kids. You are my son, but you were adopted by Charlie, and your name was changed to the same last name that we now all have." He said nothing. He suddenly smiled and asked, "Can I go out and play now?" He had not responded or questioned. I felt empty, relieved, and very sad. You see, when it's your own son of your own womb, you never know what's going on in his mind, what his emotional feelings are. My relief was due to the fact that the truth had been told, and by me; the emptiness and sadness I felt were due to the fact that he didn't reach out to me. He didn't let me know he still loved me, he wasn't showing me any forgiveness. I felt a momentary coldness and aloneness and emptiness.

It wasn't until after I divorced Charlie that the subject came about in an odd way. I'd come home the day the divorce was granted and told the children, "I've divorced your father. He will not be living with us any longer." That statement also was met with acute silence as one by one the four of them went off in their own directions except Jon, who hesitated at the front door. I went to him and he said, "You divorced Dad because of me, didn't you?" I said, "No, honey, I divorced him for all of us." He turned and went outside. I sensed no anger from any of them. I sensed no disappointment—nothing. I can only guess at what each of them was thinking and/or feeling. As I had done and been as a child, they too, had become accustomed to maintaining their self control and they too did not know how to react. They simply accepted.

Relationships are not easily defined in sentences of ten words or less. They are very intrinsically complicated. Have my children forgiven me and my indiscretions? I don't know. It is said, "Time heals all wounds," but may I add to those who may feel adversely toward me, "Time also wounds all heels."

I have done my best with what knowledge, capabilities and intuitions I have been blessed. I will always love my children and their families no matter what is behind us or what is to come. They may never understand me, yet perhaps they will one day accept me for the person I am.

THE STONE COLLECTOR

So often I've been told, "Let the child in you out—free it." I think I now have begun to do so, when I analyzed my reasons for collecting stones.

Each stone I've collected has a meaning for me, an importance. I walk along and it's as though I feel a slight pressure at the back of my head to look down, there to see a stone which I pick up, admire, and slip into my pocket until I'm home when I can place it for safe keeping. It's a trait I've rarely mentioned to anyone as I accepted it as one of my eccentricities.

Today I can harken back to my ability to work psychometry and the field of energies. Everything on this planet has some form of energy, an aura, a radiation of strength, emanating from it. As my sisters were taken from me, I kept their stones we'd warm in the oven to take to bed with us to keep us warm on those cold nights as children. I was keeping a piece of my sisters with me. Those were the first stones I began to collect. It's just continued on through the years. I don't have an extensive collection as I'm not a world traveler, but I have three very important stones from Israel. One I carry with me always, one I keep on my night stand, and the third I keep in front of the carving of Jesus. They were given to me by a beautiful friend and doctor whom I've known over many years who travels often to Israel. One never knows who may have left their emanations or energies on those or any of the trodden-upon stones I have. But when I hold any of my stones in my hands, they each give me a warm good feeling. A feeling of being loved and loving whomsoever.

Another of my eccentricities is my candles. While at home I always keep a candle lit. And when someone dear passes through the veil, a white candle is lit. Charlie never questioned my 'strange' habits, he merely accepted them as a part of my being me. At one point, there were four white candles on the television, of course when I left the house the candles were extinguished until I once again returned at which time I'd light them with a prayer that the one for whom it was meant would follow the light to God and thus be free of being earthly bound. It's strange but the candles, like the oil for the menorah for one night lasted through the eight nights, would always last the forty days for the soul to complete its journey. I always light candles after mass, usually ten or more for special indulgences and prayers for those I love and sometimes for someone I've never even met. Each saint I pray to always seems to answer my prayers. How grateful I am.

"WORKING A ROOM"

Today my son refers to my ability to mingle with people and mingle people with other people as my ability to "work a room." It's really weaving or knitting people together, somewhat as I learned to knit and sew as a little girl. It's really quite simple. You enter a group of people you may or may not know and with a quick study of a second or two you begin to merge with some. As you are talking your glance follows about the room or area until you've read most of the people there. You locate one who has somewhat isolated himself from the main group and you gradually work your way to this person. You become quickly knowledgeable regarding something of interest to him and you casually lead him out of himself into another group and with introductions and tenure you work him into the conversation and so on. Thus you "work a room;" you knit people of like type together. As you may have already surmised by this point in my book, I've always studied people and I've learned to read their body language.

Grams with Mother and 2 younger sisters with their biological father. The red-haired Scotsman whom Grams loved most until her dying day, Rob Scott.

My christening—my godfather, Dad, Mother, my godmother holding me, and my two sisters in foreground (1936).

Grams with my step-grandfather on their 25th anniversary. He was murdered—unsolved—while I was still in grammar school. Two wonderful people.

Dad's mom and dad on the porch of the farmhouse where Dad and his sibling were all born. Photo taken summer 1945. How very much I loved these two, but Grandmother passed when I was 9 years old. "All" gone, but never forgotten.

My godmother Aunt Angie, Dad's youngest sister, on her wedding day—years later she became a nun.

Myself, an aunt, and her son, my cousin. That curly hair really did me in. Age, about 5 years.

Nancy's high school graduation photo. Just looking at her face—I need say no more (1949).

Jon's christening, 1955: myself, Dad, a cousin and fiancé, godparents, and Jon.

Dad holding Jon as an infant. Not much joy—yet!—in Dad's face here.

Four generations. Dad, myself holding Jon, with Grandfather.
1956. Funny; Dad really loved the little guy.

Jon, about 2 years old.

Valley during the 1955 flood.

Valley during the 1955 flood.

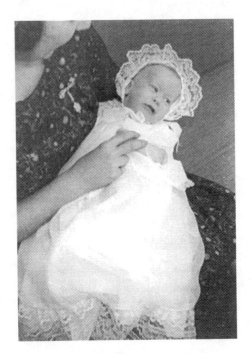

Wendy's christening (1962).

Wendy right after the accident with her foot. She amazed her doctor and everyone else.

Wendy at one of the many dog shows she worked. Just her facial expression let's you know who's in command. She won more trophies and ribbons than I can count. I'm sorry I haven't a photo of her with one of the larger group.

Brian and his beloved Irish setter "Kelly's Bridie Murphy." That dog was the bane of my existence. She got me into more cockamamy situations than I ever had gotten into on my own.

Me with Dad's "Dottie" during college years.

Nancy and myself approximately 15 years before the funerals—
still happy—still laughing. She was still beautiful!

Me with three of my four children, a year or two before the end of this part of my life.

Charlie and myself at a nephew's wedding, a couple of weeks after my heart problem and Mother's funeral, and a few months before Charlie passed.

A few months after the three funerals—worn, tired, lost and beaten.